101 ESL Activities:

For Teenagers and Adults

D1700346

Jackie Bolen +

Jennifer Booker Smith

Table of Contents

3

About the Author: Jackie Bolen

I've been teaching English in South Korea for a decade to every level and type of student and I've taught every age from kindergarten kids to adults. Most of my time has centered around teaching at two universities: five years at a science and engineering school out in the rice paddies of Chungcheongnam-Do, and four years at a major university in Busan where I now teach high level classes for students majoring in English. In my spare time, you can usually find me outside surfing, biking, hiking or on the hunt for the most delicious kimchi I can find.

In case you were wondering what my academic qualifications are, I hold a Master of Arts in Psychology. During my time in Korea I've successfully completed both the Cambridge CELTA and DELTA certification programs. With the combination of almost ten years teaching ESL/EFL learners of all ages and levels, and the more formal teaching qualifications I've obtained, I have a solid foundation on which to offer teaching advice. I truly hope that you find this book useful and would love it if you sent me an email with any questions or feedback that you might have—I'll always take the time to personally respond (jb.business.online@gmail.com).

Jackie Bolen around the Internet

ESL Speaking (www.eslspeaking.org)

Jackie Bolen (www.jackiebolen.com)

Twitter: @bolen_jackie

Email: jb.business.online@gmail.com

Other books on Amazon: www.amazon.com/author/jackiebolen

About the Author: Jennifer Booker Smith

I have a Master of Education in TESOL and have spent fifteen years teaching students of all ages in Korea, from two-year-old preschoolers barely out of diapers to businessmen and even a semester as a teacher trainer at an education university. However, my greatest love is the middle primary grades—I left a fairly cushy teacher trainer position to return to the elementary classroom. In that age group, I've taught all ability levels from false beginner to near-native returnees.

During my time in the classroom, I've created countless board and card games and other resources. In this book, you'll find some of the vocabulary activities that I have used successfully (I've tried plenty which weren't successful!) in a variety of settings; these are the ones I've used again and again because they actually work.

When I'm not teaching, like Jackie, you can often find me hiking. I've taken up running recently and will soon be running my third half marathon. Teaching takes up a lot more "free" time than non-teachers will ever realize, so it's important to recharge the batteries and being outside is my favorite way to do just that.

You can get in touch with me by emailing jenniferteacher@gmail.com. I'd love to hear from you and help you with your classes in any way that I can.

4 Skills-Higher Level

Agony Aunt

Skills: Listening/Speaking/Reading

Time: 15-20 minutes

Level: High-beginner to Advanced

Materials: Printed advice column questions and answers

This activity will get your students talking because everyone knows how to solve other people's problems! If your students are a bit more advanced, you can use actual advice columns. These can easily be found by searching on the Internet for "advice column" etc. The lower the students' level, the more you'll need to grade the language, or you can write your own advice column.

I've done several variations of this activity and it has always been a hit. I begin with an introduction that shows a few advice column letters and answers. Discuss them a bit—most students will be familiar with the concept. Then, give your students a copy of a letter (not the same one from the introduction).

Version 1:

All the students receive the same letter. Each person has 3-8 minutes (depending on the level) to come up with some advice (separately). The class has a short discussion about what advice each person would give and why. You can also have students discuss their advice in small groups if you have a larger class.

Version 2:

All the students (small classes) or groups (big classes) receive a different letter. As above, each person/group is given time to read and think of some advice. You can begin the discussion time by having each person quickly summarize the problem they have read about, then give some advice and discuss that.

Teaching Tip:

If you are familiar with local celebrities popular with your students, you can use current gossip to spice up the lesson. If X pop star has just had a public breakup, write a letter from that person asking for help getting back together, finding a new boyfriend, etc. For the men, a rumor of a football star being traded works well to get advice on how to improve that player's game.

Procedure:

1. Show some level-appropriate advice column letters. Read them together and discuss.

Version 1:

1. All students get the same letter (not one from the introduction).

2. Each person has to read the letter and come up with some advice (separately).

3. Discuss each person's advice.

Version 2:

1. The students get different letters.

2. Give some time to read the letter and come up with some advice.

3. Discuss the problems and their advice.

Infographic Presentation

Skills: Reading/Writing/Speaking/Listening

Time: 1+ hour

Level: High-Beginner to Advanced

Materials: Internet access, PowerPoint

Optional Materials: Video camera

Presentations are a regular feature of ESL classes, but your student may get overwhelmed at the thought of first creating and then presenting a full-length speech. Infographics have become a common way of presenting information, and your student can create and use one to provide the "meat" of an informative oral presentation. This will also provide an opportunity to research a topic in English. If your student works in an office, he or she is likely to use PowerPoint at work, so the combination of something familiar (PPT) with something new (English presentation) should reduce stress.

Have your student choose a topic of interest to them that has several data points. For example, if he/she has a favorite team, he/she can find the team's current ranking, average points per game, number of championships, and so on to populate the infographic. The student should begin the project by researching several data points and finding an image or two online to use for decoration.

To create the infographic, the student will need to reset the margins to create the long, narrow look of an infographic. This is done by choosing a blank layout and changing the slide from landscape to portrait then adjusting the margins. Start with 10"/25cm by 30"/75cm and adjust if necessary. Your student can use images, Smart Art, and/or charts to present the data he/she will report. However, you may want to give your student a time limit for choosing a layout or have him/her make a sketch before opening PowerPoint, because the number of

9

options can become a time waster.

Once the layout has been chosen, your student will need to fill in the data. If he/she is using charts, Excel will automatically to fill them in. Don't worry, it's pretty self-explanatory and the end result is right there for the student to see while working. Once the images are all in place, the student should add a brief explanation of each image. All images and text boxes can be resized, and the entire slide can be resized by adjusting the margins, if there is more (or less) information than expected.

When the student is satisfied with the infographic, it can be saved as a JPEG. This will probably have taken an entire lesson, so the presentation will be in the next lesson. You should tailor the focus of the presentation to your student's level and needs. A lower-level student may just need to practice speaking without a script. Higher-level students may need to practice the use of gestures or inflection.

For the presentation of the infographic, pull up the saved image and have the student sit or stand next to the computer to present the data to you. A lower-level student may do best seated next to you with both of you looking at the screen. Being able to look at the image (and not having you looking directly at your student) should reduce quite a bit of stress. After doing several presentation activities, the student's confidence will hopefully increase and he/she won't need such modifications.

Teaching Tips:

If your student does not use PowerPoint at work and is not familiar with it (or if you do not want to spend an entire lesson making an infographic), you may want to have the student find an existing infographic online to present.

A video of the presentation can be helpful for your student. When students see and hear themselves, they can more easily see the areas that need improvement.

Procedure:

1. Have your student choose a topic of interest that would have several data points to research and present.

2. Have the student make a sketch of the planned infographic.

3. Using PowerPoint, have the student make the infographic (use a blank layout, in portrait, with the margins set to 10"/25cm by 30"/75cm).

4. In the next lesson, have the student present the infographic to you. According to the student's level, have him/her focus on speaking without a script, using gestures, or inflection, etc.

5. Review the presentation.

Interesting Story and Questions

Skills: Writing/Reading/Speaking/Listening

Time: 15-30 minutes

Level: Advanced

Materials: None

Have students write something interesting. Some examples you can use are: most embarrassing moment, scariest thing you've ever done, your dream for the future, etc. Base it on whatever you are studying in class. Then, distribute the stories to other people in the class. They have to go around the class, finding the person whose story they have by asking questions. Once they find that person, they have to ask three interesting questions about the story.

Teaching Tips:

Emphasize to students that they are to practice asking good *full-sentence* questions. For example, "USA?" is not a good question, while, "Did you study abroad in the USA?" is much better. Also emphasize that students should think of interesting follow-up questions that expand upon their knowledge about that situation. This involves reading carefully so they can avoid asking about things that are already mentioned. You can give your students a couple of minutes before the activity starts to write down a few questions based on the paper they received to help facilitate this.

This activity provides an excellent opportunity for your students to work on reported speech. This is something that high level students are often surprisingly weak at. If you have a small class (fewer than 10), students can report what they learned about their partner to everyone. If larger, students can tell their seating partner what they learned. For example, students might say something like, "I talked to Min-Ji. She told me that she got in a car accident last year. She said that it was really scary, but thankfully nobody got injured seriously. "

Procedure:

1. Have students write an interesting story based on a certain topic. Adjust for length and difficultly depending on your students.

2. Collect stories and redistribute them—one per student, making sure a student does not get their own story.

3. Students go around the class asking people if they have their story. For example, "Did you get in a car accident when you were little?"

4. When they find the person, they must ask them three interesting follow-up questions about it.

5. Do the optional variation of having students tell other people what they learned in order to practice using reported speech.

Problem and Advice

Skills: Reading/Writing/Speaking/Listening

Time: 30-40 minutes

Level: Intermediate to Advanced

Materials: None

This is an excellent activity for studying should/shouldn't and better/better not. Write down a problem such as a high school student studying for the University Entrance Exam who is exhausted and can't sleep at night. Have the students prepare some advice for that person in groups of 2-4. When everyone is ready, have the groups share their answers with the class. The most helpful and clear advice gets a prize of some kind; you can either choose the winner or have the class vote on it.

Teaching Tips:

This also makes an excellent homework activity if you get the students to make a video talking about their advice for a certain problem. To make it even more fun, I'll often make my own video of the problem and put it up on *YouTube* for them to watch, either in class or at home. I usually ham it up a bit and add some drama and may perhaps even have a friend make a guest appearance. Students love seeing their teacher on *YouTube*!

Giving some advice or an opinion in a polite way is an important functional skill that students need to learn and this activity is particularly helpful for that. It's worthwhile to spend some time talking about how to make your advice more, or less, polite depending on the circumstance.

Procedure:

1. Think of a problem of some kind, depending on the topic being studied and the level of the students.

2. Ask students to give some advice to that person. Give them time to prepare their presentation in small groups.

3. Each team does a short presentation in front of the class sharing the advice that they came up with. You choose the best, or have the class vote on it.

Secret Person

Skills: Writing/Reading/Speaking/Listening

Time: 20-30 minutes

Level: Intermediate to Advanced

Materials: None

This is the perfect activity for using "be" statements in the past tense. Have students think of two dead people and write down when he was born/where he was from, why he was famous, how he died, and one or two more interesting things. Then, put the students into small groups of 4-5 to play together. The first student gives the student to the right of them the first hint and they get one guess. If correct that student gets a point and goes next, starting with the person on their right. If incorrect, the first student gives the next hint to the next person to the right and they get a guess. This pattern continues until the correct answer is guessed.

Teaching Tips:

You can play this game with the whole class, but it's better in small groups because it's far more student-centered. Of course, you should do a demonstration first with the whole class before you let them play together.

Many students pick the same two or three people, depending on the country where you are teaching. I avoid this situation by using those people as my examples. I'll say something like, "You need to pick two dead people, for example, Michael Jackson and Kim Jong II." In Korea, a couple more people you could ban are Lee Sun Shin and King Sejong!

Procedure:

1. Do a demonstration for the students first. Think of a dead person. Give some hints, such as when he was born, where he was from, why he was famous, etc.

2. Have the students guess who the person is after each hint.

3. Put students into small groups and have them choose two dead people and write some hints about him/her. Giving around 5-6 hints is best. Be sure to start with the hardest ones

and get to the easiest ones at the end.

4. The students do rock-scissor-paper and the winner goes first. The winner gives the person to his/her right the most difficult hint and then that person gets one guess. If correct, the person on the right gets a point and the game continues with his/her secret person. He/she starts with the person on his/her right. If incorrect, the winner gives the next student to the right in the circle the next hint and they get one guess. It continues until the correct guess is given.

Speaking Bingo

Skills: Speaking/Listening/Writing

Time: 20-30 minutes

Level: High-Beginner to Advanced

Materials: Blank "Bingo" grids, or blank paper

This is a very fun activity that teenagers as well as university students seem to love. Have a list of about 30 vocabulary words that you've been studying. If you use fewer, the game will be over very quickly. Give the students a pre-made Bingo Grid, or have them draw a 5x5 grid. Then the students fill in the grid randomly from the list of words on the board or PowerPoint. Then, choose someone to go first (rock-scissor-paper, draw numbers out of a hat, according to the attendance sheet, etc.). The first student describes a word, but doesn't actually say the word. The next person describes another word and on it goes, just like a regular Bingo game, but the students are speaking the whole time. You can do variations, such as "1 line," "2 lines," "X-Bingo" and "Blackout." This variation works best in smaller classes of ten or less.

In bigger classes, you can describe the words but it becomes solely a listening and writing exercise instead of a speaking one. Another way to do it would be to put students in small groups of 4-6 to play together; there are two benefits—there's more student talking time and it becomes more of a strategic game because each student can keep an eye on their opponent's boards.

Teaching Tips:

One important strategy to increase fluency that our students need to practice is producing synonyms of a word they don't know, or can't remember the exact word that they want. This Bingo game is an excellent way to focus on this.

This game requires absolutely no prep-time if you are given a class at the last minute and need something to fill the time. Simply ask the students what they've been studying the past few days or weeks and if they say, "animals," then ask them to tell you all the animals they know and write them on the board, and that will form the list they have to choose from as they prepare their boards.

Ask the students to use a highlighter or just an "x" over the words instead of scribbling it out entirely with their pens. This way, you are able to check their answers in case of a Bingo.

Procedure:

1. Prepare blank Bingo grid photocopies beforehand (or students can draw their own on paper), as well as a list of vocab words (PowerPoint works well).

2. Students fill in the Bingo grid with their chosen words.

3. The first student chooses a word and describes it, using hints but not the word itself. You can choose the order of who describes words any number of ways: drawing numbers, seating arrangement, alphabetical order, etc.

4. All students cross off that word if they have it on their Bingo grid. The next student describes a word and so on.

5. The first student to get one line is the winner. The next winner is two lines, then "X", and then "blackout." My rule is that you can't win more than one round.

Survey Activities

Skills: Speaking/Listening/Writing/Reading

Time: 15-30 minutes

Level: High-Beginner to Advanced

Materials: Survey handout

Give the students a sheet of paper with some questions and tell them they need to find one of their classmates who will fit each slot. My general rule is that one question equals around two minutes for intermediate to advanced students so 10 questions would equal a 20 minute activity; it's one minute per question for beginners because they will not be as good at asking follow-up questions. The kinds of questions you could put on your paper include things like: "Do you travel sometimes?" or, "Are you a university student?" Then, if their partner answers yes (encourage students to answer in full sentences!), they write down their partner's name and ask them one (beginner) or two (intermediate to advanced) more questions to elicit some extra information. They can only ask each classmate one question. If their partner's answer is no, they should choose another question to ask them.

Prep the activity well before you turn students loose by saying what you're looking for: only speaking English, everybody standing up, talking to everybody in mostly full sentences, writing the answers in English. Get a student to ask you one of the questions first and then ask a student one of the questions so your students have two models of what they need to do. Here is a survey that I would use on the first day of class:

Get to Know Each Other Survey

Name	Do you _____? Are you _____?	Extra Information (W/H _____?)
	from outside this city	
	in third year	
	play sports	
	live alone	
	eat pizza a lot	
	an only child	
	play sports	
	have a part time job	
	have a boyfriend or girlfriend	
	like horror movies	
	in second year	
	take the subway to school	

	think English is the best subject	
	enjoying this class	
	love your school	
	like studying English	

Teaching Tips:

Surveys are an excellent way for students to practice some important speaking sub-skills, especially responding appropriately based on what their partner tells them. For example, if they are surprised they could respond with, "Really?" If in agreement, they could say, "Yeah, me too." If in strong disagreement, they could say something like, "Wow! Why do you think that?" You could even put three categories on the board for "Agree", "Disagree" and "Surprise" and elicit a few ideas from the students about appropriate things they could say in response to a statement.

Another important speaking sub-skill is turn taking. I emphasize to my students that there are times when in-depth and lengthy discourses are necessary (a presentation) but doing a survey activity like this mimics small talk. In small talk, the keys are to listen well, ask some interesting questions and follow-up questions, give short, concise answers and not to ramble. I will sometimes give my students an example of a rambling answer and they usually find it really funny, but I hope that they get the point too!

Procedure:

1. Prepare the survey, based on whatever you are studying.

2. Hand out surveys and write up one or two of the question on the board, making it look the same as the handout. Do two example questions with students, one with you asking a student a question and vice-versa for the second one.

3. Students stand up and talk to one classmate asking them one question (any order is okay). If the answer is "yes," they write in the name and ask a follow-up question. They can write one or two words in the appropriate slot based on the answer their partner gave them.

4. If the answer is no, they must ask another question from the survey until they get a "yes."

5. The pair splits up and each student finds a new partner to talk to.

6. The activity continues until the allotted time is finished.

4 Skills-Lower Level

Ball Toss

Skills: Reading/Writing/Speaking/Listening

Time: 5-10 minutes

Level: Beginner to Intermediate

Materials: Lightweight ball (such as a beach ball) with questions written on it

This game has many variations. One variation I have used with great success is writing questions on a beach ball. I use a white board marker to write on the ball, but let it dry thoroughly before class, so it doesn't smudge but it can be washed clean and reused with different questions later. Students gently toss the ball to one another and read aloud and answer the question under their right thumb. A more complex variation is: Student A reads/asks the question, tosses the ball to Student B, who answers that question, then asks the question under their right thumb, and tosses the ball to Student C, who answers Student B's question.

If it's a "getting to know you" activity, use questions to elicit name, age, and basic information. Otherwise, it can be used to practice likes/dislikes, 5 W/H-questions, etc. It is quite a versatile activity and can be used with just about anything that you're studying.

If you don't have a ball handy, you can crumple up a piece of paper to use as a ball. Ask a question and toss the ball to a student. That student must answer and ask a question (the same question for true beginners or related question, if higher level), then toss the "ball" to the next student. If you want the students to ask different questions, you should give them a topic (daily routine, hobbies, etc.) or grammar pattern to use.

If you want to make sure all students have equal turns, have students sit down after catching the ball. If you have more than 10-12 students in your class, you may want to divide them into groups, each with their own ball, so students aren't waiting long periods between turns. This will also increase student talking time.

Teaching Tips:

At the end, you may want to ask students questions about other students' answers. Let students know before they begin that they need to listen closely to each other's answers. This will make them more likely to pay attention between their own turns and, of course, provide additional listening and speaking practice.

Generally, this activity can be used with all ages. You can even use it with younger students as long as their ability is high enough to answer the questions. The same for class size: you can use it for larger classes, as long as their level is move advanced, simply because they will be better suited to working in small groups with less attention needed from you. If you have a class of 30 beginners, you might want to simply toss the ball and ask a question, rather than require them to read it, and have each student repeat the same question as they toss the ball. After 10-12 students have asked and answered the same question, take the ball and toss it to a different student, asking a new question.

Procedure:

1. Prepare a beach ball by writing questions on it. Allow enough time for the ink to dry before class. Low prep version: crumple up a piece of scrap paper with the questions written on it.

2. Have students stand in a circle (as much as possible). If your class is large, divide students into groups of 10-12.

Variation A:

When a student catches the ball, they must read out the question under their right thumb. They answer their own question and toss the ball to another student.

Variation B:

When Student A catches the ball, they ask the question under their right thumb to Student B. When Student B answers, A tosses them the ball. Student B asks Student C the question under their right thumb and so on.

No Prep Variation:

The teacher asks a question and tosses the ball to Student A. Student A answers, asks Student B a question, and tosses them the ball.

Dialogue Substitution

Skills: Reading/Listening/Speaking

Time: 10-15 minutes

Level: Beginner to Intermediate

Materials: PowerPoint or handouts of photocopied textbook dialogue with parts removed.

Lower-level text books contain many dialogues but their effectiveness is reduced when students don't have to listen to their partner in order to successfully complete their role. An easy solution to this is to provide the dialogues with key elements missing. Students then have to listen in order to respond appropriately. Dialogues are an excellent way for students to see how new vocabulary is used in real-life situations.

You may want or need to scaffold this activity by providing a list of possible words, phrases, or grammar patterns that could be used to fill the gaps. Alternatively, you can make the activity more difficult or realistic by allowing students to complete the dialogue using any language that makes sense, even if it hasn't been presented in that lesson.

This activity is also useful for reviewing some basic conversation strategies: asking a speaker to repeat what he/she has said, or asking for clarification (as well as others). This is an area where students may need a bit of scaffolding, such as a few ways to politely ask others to repeat themselves:

One more time, please?

Sorry, I didn't understand.

Also, remind students that when they speak to someone, they should be looking at the person, rather than at a handout or screen.

Procedure:

1. Before class, scan or photocopy a textbook dialogue with the target language removed.

2. Optionally, create a list of possible words or phrases that students can use to complete the dialogue or, encourage students to use other words or phrases that will fit the target language. Also, introduce any language needed for practicing communication strategies (see above).

3. Divide students into pairs and have them take turns being A and B.

4. To extend the activity, have students change partners and repeat the dialogue, using different words to create a new conversation.

Dictogloss

Skills: Speaking/Listening

Time: 10-15 minutes

Level: Intermediate to Advanced

Materials: A short story

This is a simple activity for higher level students that helps them practice their listening and memory skills, as well as substituting vocabulary words if the original word is no longer accessible to them. You can find a short, interesting story of some kind or make up one yourself. I've used various things from children's stories to a story about something I did on the weekend. Just about anything can work.

Tell the story 1-3 times, depending on the student level and of course you can also vary your speaking speed to make this activity easier or harder. Once you are done telling the story, students will have to go in groups of 2-3 to retell the story. Emphasize that they won't be able to recreate the exact story that you told, but that they should try their best to keep the meaning the same. Each team can pair up with another team to compare. Then, tell the original story again so students can see how they did.

This activity works well as a writing activity too.

Teaching Tips:

It's very helpful for students to compare answers with a partner before they have to say anything in front of the class so be sure to put them in partners or groups of three to work together on this activity. It's useful for the weaker students to have a stronger student getting them up to speed. It also gives students confidence that they're on the right track and they're less nervous to share their answers with the class.

If you use something "scandalous," it will make the activity a lot more fun! Of course, it should still be appropriate so just picture your boss observing your class to decide if you should use it or not.

Procedure:

1. Prepare a short story which you'll read to your students.

2. Put students in groups of two or three and read the story to them.

3. Students try to remember the details of the story and compare with their group. I usually only allow them to do this by speaking.

4. Read the story again and students attempt to recreate the story more closely, again by speaking.

5. Read the story again (depending on level and difficulty of story) and students again attempt to recreate it, even more closely.

6. Elicit a couple of teams to tell their story to the class (in a small class). Or, put two teams together and they tell their stories to each other (in a larger class).

7. Read the story one final time for students to compare their own versions

Do you like to _____?

Skills: Speaking/Listening

Time: 15 minutes

Level: Intermediate

Materials: Strips of paper (or students can make their own)

Give each student five strips of paper. On each piece of paper they write something interesting about themselves. Then, collect them, mix them up and distribute them back to your students (three per student). At this point, everyone stands up and goes around the class asking questions to try to find the owner for each paper that they have. If someone is done early, you can give them another paper from the reserve pile that you have.

For example,

"Did you go to _____ middle school?"

"Do you have a twin brother?"

"Do you love to play soccer?"

Teaching Tip:

Students need to write down *interesting and unique* things about themselves. For example, "I go to XYZ university" is something that every other student in the class will say yes to so it is not a good thing to use.

Procedure:

1. Give students five strips of paper (or they provide their own).

2. Students write down one interesting thing about themselves on each paper.

3. Collect papers and redistribute (three per student).

4. Students stand up and go around the class, asking their classmates, "Do you have a twin brother?" "Can you play the piano really well?" based on what is on their papers.

5. If it's a match, they get one point and that paper is "finished." Optionally, you can require higher level students to ask 1-3 follow-up questions before they get a point.

6. If a student finds all their matches, they can get one or two more papers from your reserve pile.

-er Dictionary Activity

Skill: Reading/Writing/Speaking/Listening

Time: 10+ minutes

Level: Beginner

Materials: Worksheet

Students learn early on that –er refers to a person who does something. Examples include, teacher, writer, baker, etc. However, nouns ending in –er can refer to people, animals, or objects or can have multiple meanings involving a combination of the above. The activity will reinforce the need to be cautious with general rules in English while providing dictionary practice.

Begin by preparing a list of nouns ending with –er. If you would like this to be a brief activity, limit it to about five words. The more words you include, the longer the activity will be. Have three columns beside the list for students to tick if the word refers to a person, animal, and/or object. Students should use their dictionaries to determine which categories each word belongs to.

Here are enough –er words for an entire class period:

Blender, Bumper, Buyer

Cadaver, Canister, Cleaner, Coaster, Customer

Diver, Dozer, Driver

Fryer

Hipster

Oyster

Passenger, Pitcher, Planner, Player

Ringer, Roster

Scanner, Sticker, Stinger

Walker

To add a speaking element, have students work with partners after filling in their answers. Partners should take turns asking and answering questions about the words. For example, "A person who bakes is a baker. Is a person who cooks a cooker?"

Teaching Tips:

Depending on the level of the class, you can allow students to defend answers they may come up with, such as, "A banner is a person who bans," or simply explain that it is a logical conclusion, but that English is not always logical.

This may be a good time to review "a person who. . ." and "a thing that. . ."

Procedure:

1. In advance, prepare a worksheet with a list of nouns ending in –er with tickbox columns for

person, animal, and object. Also, at least one class beforehand, instruct students to bring their dictionaries on the appropriate date if you do not have class sets.

2. Explain to students that although they know that nouns ending in –er are people, -er words can also refer to animals and objects.

3. Have students use their dictionaries to categorize each word on the list as person, animal, and/or object.

4. When students have looked up all the words, have them work with a partner asking and answering questions about the words. For example, "Is a walker a person who walks?" (Answer: "Yes, and also something that helps people walk.")

Flyer Time

Skills: Speaking/Listening

Time: 10+ minutes

Level: Beginner to Intermediate

Materials: Prepared flyers/ads and questions

This activity is used to practice answering questions with a visual aid. While your students are unlikely to be asked which bands are playing at X festival, they may need to answer questions about a presentation or report in English. In advance, prepare several event flyers or ads and questions. Prepare some questions that have the answers clearly stated:
"What time will _____ begin?"
"Where will this take place?"

Also include some questions that require the students to think about the event and use existing knowledge:
"Who do you think will be attending this event?"
"Will attendees need to do anything in advance?" (For example, make a reservation or buy tickets)

In class, give the flyer to your students and ask them to use it to answer your questions. Explain that not all of the answers are stated explicitly.

Teaching Tip:

The questions should mostly be content questions with a few purpose questions. The more advanced your students are, the more questions you should ask that are not explicitly answered.

Procedure:

1. In advance, prepare several event flyers and questions (see above for examples) for your student to answer using the flyers.

2. Let your students know that not all questions are explicitly answered on the flyer.

3. Have your students use the flyer to answer the questions.

4. Ask the questions. Do not let your students read the answers word for word.

Is that Sentence Correct?

Skills: Listening/Speaking/Reading/Writing

Time: 10-20 minutes

Level: Beginner to Advanced

Materials: Blank paper, vocabulary words

This is a sneaky way to get your students to make grammatically correct sentences using the target vocabulary. Start off by giving your students 5-6 vocabulary words. They should be words that the students are quite familiar with already. The challenge in this activity is not the actual word; it's using it in a sentence. Give the students five minutes to make some sentences using those words (one sentence per word). Do not offer any assistance or correct any errors. You can also make some sentences using the same (or different, but familiar to the student) vocabulary words. Some of them should be correct while some of them should be incorrect.

The first student reads his/her first sentence. Discuss whether it is correct or incorrect and why. Read your first sentence and have a brief discussion about whether it is correct or incorrect. The activity continues until all the sentences are done. If you have a larger class (more than six students), you can put students into groups of 3-4 and have them make sentences together.

Procedure:

1. Give the students a few vocabulary words (and, as the teacher, you can use the same words or different words that the students are familiar with).

2. Instruct the students to write one sentence per word while you do the same with your words. Make some sentences correct and some incorrect.

3. Take turns reading sentences and discussing whether they are correct or incorrect.

Just Fill in This Form, Please

Skills: Reading/Writing/Speaking/Listening

Time: 5-20 minutes

Level: Beginner to Intermediate

Materials: Application form

Filling in forms is an often-overlooked skill for language learners, but life is full of forms. To prepare for this activity, talk to your students in advance to find out what kinds of forms they have to fill out in English. Some possibilities include customs and immigration forms when traveling, banking documents, registration paperwork (such as for a doctor or a credit card) and job applications. Whatever your students need, a quick Google search should turn up a generic example you can use in class.

Most forms have a fair bit of overlap in terms of requested information, so your students should get a quick boost of confidence, but there may be important differences in how dates and addresses are written compared to their first language. Any such variations can be quickly learned, and you can move along to the more challenging sections. The challenges to your students will be in the areas of vocabulary used on forms as well as writing responses in the way expected by those who collect the forms.

You can do this as a writing activity, discussing each section with your students, or you can complete the forms as a role play. For the role play, make two copies of the blank form so that students working in pairs can take turns playing the "information collector" and the "subject."

Procedure:

1. In advance, find out what kinds of forms your students need to fill out in English

2. Find examples online and print two copies of each form you want to use.

3. Have your students take turns playing the parts of the "information collector" and the "subject."

Q&A

Skills: Speaking/Listening/Reading/Writing

Time: 10 minutes

Level: Beginner to Intermediate

Materials: None

This is a simple variation on having students make example sentences using their vocabulary list. Students work in pairs of teams, creating a list of WH questions (to avoid yes/no answers) using their vocabulary words. When they have five questions, teams should alternate asking a question to another team and answering the other team's questions.

You can extend the activity with some reported speech practice, which will give teams an incentive to listen to the responses to their questions.

Procedure:

1. Divide students into an even number of teams of 2-4. Then pair two teams together.

2. Give students a few minutes to create five WH questions using their vocabulary words.

3. Have the paired teams alternate asking and answering each other's questions.

4. Optionally, extend the activity by having teams briefly report the other team's answers.

Rock-Scissor-Paper

Skills: Reading/Writing/Speaking/Listening

Time: 20 minutes

Level: Beginner to Intermediate

Materials: Question and answer papers (5 per student)

This is an excellent review activity to do before a test for lower level classes where there are well-defined, closed type questions and answers. On separate papers, make matching questions and answers. Give each student five random papers with a mix of both questions and answers. They have to walk around the class to find their "match." Once they do, they can rock-scissor-paper and the winner takes both papers and those papers are "out." In order to increase student talking time, my rule is that students cannot read each other's papers but must find the matching papers only through speaking. If I see students reading, I enforce a penalty of some kind, where I usually take away one of their matches. The students with the most points (matches) after a certain period of time are the winners.

Teaching Tip:

Try to design questions that have unambiguous questions and answers. I mean that each question should have one very specific answer and not be possible for other papers. Make sure you do a demonstration with a couple examples before you start so your students understand the game. I'll usually set aside a couple of matches for my demo and arrange it so that two good students get one part, while I keep the corresponding one. Then I "find" the matches.

Procedure:

1. Prepare matching question and answer papers using unambiguous questions and answers. Cut them out into single strips of paper (questions and answers are separate).

2. Give each student five random papers, in a mix of questions and answers.

3. Students walk around the class, finding their "match." They can do this only by speaking and not by reading each other's papers.

4. Once they find a match, they do rock-scissor-paper.

5. The winner keeps both papers and that set is finished.

6. The winner is the student with the most sets after the allotted time. If there are more than two or three students who are the "winners," you can reduce this by having a final rock-scissor-paper showdown.

7. Check carefully at the end of the game to ensure that papers are indeed matches. It can be a good teachable moment to explain why a potential match is incorrect if a mistake is made.

Role-plays

Skills: Writing/Reading/Speaking/Listening

Time Required: 20-40 minutes

Level: Beginner to Intermediate

Materials: None

Partner role-plays are an excellent way to get students practicing using new vocabulary in a real-life context. Give the students a conversation starter to get them going. For example, if you're talking about *feelings* in class that day, you can use:

A: Hey _____, how are you doing?

B: I'm great, how are you?

A: I'm _____ (sad, embarrassed, angry, bored, etc.). ***Anything besides, "I'm fine, thank you, and you?" is good. ***

B: Oh? What's wrong?

A: _____.

B: _____.

Another context that I often use this activity with is *illness or injury*. For example:

A: Hey _____, you don't look (sound) so good! What's wrong?

B: Oh yeah, I'm not good. I _____.

A: Really? _____.

B: _____.

A: _____.

One final context that I use this with is *excuses*. For example:

A: Hey _____, you're _____ minutes late!

B: I'm really sorry. I've been/I had to _____.

A: Hmmm . . . _____.

Give the students about ten minutes to write the conversation with their partner. You can adjust the number of lines and how detailed of a starter you give to suit the ability level of your students. For lower-level students, it can be helpful to have a word bank relevant to the context on the whiteboard so that the writing portion of this activity doesn't get too long (you can also provide them with a detailed, fill-in-the-blank script). Then, the students memorize their conversation (no papers when speaking!), and do a role-play in front of their classmates if you have a small class of fewer than ten. Remember that you should try to maximize the amount of time students are talking. If you have a larger class, there are a few different ways to handle this. You could get pairs to come up to your desk and show you their conversation while the other students are working on something else, you could use it as a speaking test of some kind, each pair could join with one or two other groups and perform for them, or finally you could have students make a video of themselves and send you the link or upload it to *YouTube*.

I really like this activity because it's perfect for lower-level students who want to practice "conversation" but don't quite have the skills to do this on their own, and it's also a good way to force your advanced students to use some new grammar or vocabulary that you're teaching.

Teaching Tips:

Having your students make conversations is very useful for practicing functional language and speaking sub-skills. I usually choose one or two functions to mention when I'm giving the instructions for the activity and provide a bit of coaching and language input surrounding that, depending on the level—beginners will need more help.

The functions that fit particularly well with partner conversations include agreeing, disagreeing, apologizing, and asking advice. The sub-skills that you can emphasize are things like turn-taking, initiating a conversation, speaking for an appropriate length of time, stress and intonation, responding (really?), and cohesive devices, particularly noun pronoun reference: A: I saw a movie last night. B: Which one did you see? A. I saw Iron Man. It was good.

This is one of the most useful things you can do in your conversation classes, especially for beginner or intermediate students so make sure you try it out at least once or twice over the course of a semester. It gives your students a chance to have a real conversation which will build a lot of confidence but they won't have the pressure of coming up with something to say on the spot. That said, it gets boring if you do this every class; I generally do it about once a month for a class that meets twice a week over the course of a semester.

Procedure:

1. Prepare a conversation starter based on what you are teaching.

2. (Optional) Pre-teach some language that students could use, if you haven't done that already in your lesson.

3. Write the conversation starter on the whiteboard, PowerPoint, or on a handout.

4. Have students complete the conversation in pairs. Then, they must prepare to speak by memorizing and adding in stress and intonation. You could give some individual help to each pair to assist them in knowing what to stress and how to do it.

5. Have students stand up and "perform" their conversation if you have a small class. In larger

classes, there are a few other options (see above).

6. Reward teams for interesting conversations, good acting (no reading), and correct use of grammar/vocabulary that you were teaching that day.

Running Dictation

Skills: Writing/Listening/Speaking/Reading

Time: 15 minutes

Level: Beginner to Advanced

Materials: The "dictation" + some way to attach it to the walls or board.

This is one of my favorite activities which covers reading, writing, listening and speaking. There are a wide variety of English styles you can choose: poems, song lyrics, a short story, famous quotes—the list is almost limitless. For example, you might make up a story or conversation a few sentences long (no more than ten). Put each sentence on a strip of paper, and you can also put another strip of paper on top to prevent cheating. Put these around the classroom in various locations.

The students will be in teams of two. One person is the reader and one is the writer. The reader gets up and reads a bit of the passage and comes and tells it to the writer. They go back to remember more of it and so on and so on. At the end, the students have to put the song or conversation in order. If you have beginner students, make sure it's obvious enough what the correct order should be. Intermediate and advanced students can handle something with a bit of ambiguity. When they're done, I'll check their writing and if there aren't many mistakes plus the order is correct, that team is the winner. How many mistakes you allow depends on the level of your students.

Tell your students before the activity starts that standing at the strip of paper and then yelling to their partner instead of walking over to them is not allowed or they will be disqualified.

Teaching Tips:

Make sure you let your students know what cheating is (yelling, the "reader/speaker" touching the pen, using their phone camera) and if that happens their team will automatically be disqualified.

Make sure you move beyond simply dictating the sentences down onto the paper into dealing with meaning as well. You can do this by requiring students to put the conversation, song or poem in the correct order. They can simply write "1, 2, 3, 4" beside each sentence instead of re-writing them. Make sure whatever you choose has some sort of logical order to it. Alternatively, if you choose something that doesn't really have an order, you could skip this step.

Procedure:

1. Prepare a simple story or conversation and put each sentence on a strip of paper.

2. Put the papers around the classroom on the wall, equally spaced out.

3. Divide the students into pairs: one writer and one reader.

4. The reader stands up, walks to the station and reads a paper, then goes back to the writer and tells what they read to the writer, who must write it. The reader can go back to a single paper as many times as required.

5. This procedure of reading, speaking, listening, and writing continues until the team has all the sentences down on their paper.

6. The two students put the story or conversation in the correct order.

7. The teacher can check for accuracy and meaning and decide if it's acceptable, or not.

Sentence Substitution Ladder

Skills: Speaking/Listening/Writing (optional)

Time: 5-20 minutes

Level: High-Beginner to Low-Intermediate

Materials: Sentences

This is a simple activity to get students to think about how they can use the words they know. They will be very familiar with substitution drills, but this goes one step further to get lower-level students comfortable with using the language a bit more creatively. They have the knowledge, but they may need a push to use it.

Give the class a sentence practicing familiar categories of words (places, activities, etc.) and a familiar grammatical structure. Then, instruct him/her to change one word at a time to make a new sentence. Each position must be changed one time (as in, first word, second word, etc.), but it doesn't have to be done in order. Optionally, you can have them write the new sentences.

An example ladder would be:

Original sentence: I saw a black cat walk under a ladder.

I saw an orange cat walk under a ladder.

We saw an orange cat walk under a ladder.

We saw an orange cat run under a ladder.

We saw an orange cat run under the bed.

We saw an orange cat run to the bed.

We heard an orange cat run to the bed.

We heard an orange dog run to the bed.

Teaching Tip:

Unless you want to specifically target articles and numbers, you can consider noun phrases as a single unit.

Procedure:

1. In advance, prepare several sentences using familiar categories of words (places, activities, etc.) and a familiar grammatical structure.

2. Have the students change one word at a time to make a new sentence.

3. Each position must be changed one time (as in, first word, second word, etc.), but it doesn't have to be done in order.

38

Word Association

Skills: Reading/Writing/Listening/Speaking

Time: 5 minutes

Level: Beginner to Advanced

Materials: Whiteboard and markers or butcher (A3) paper and pens

To introduce a new vocabulary word, write it in the middle of the board or paper and have students take turns adding as many words or images related to that word as possible. For large classes, have students work in groups with separate pieces of paper taped to the wall or the top of the table/grouped desks. After a given amount of time (2-3 minutes, or when you see no one is adding anything new), discuss their answers.

Teaching Tips:

If you're using butcher paper (or A3 in a pinch), prepare in advance by taping it to the wall unless students will be working at their desks. If students will be working at their desks, write the word on each table's page in advance, but don't hand them out, until you have given your instructions.

Procedure:

1. Write a single new vocabulary word on the whiteboard or butcher paper.

2. Have students take turns adding as many words or images related to that word as possible.

3. After 2-3 minutes (or less, if no one is adding anything new), discuss their answers.

Listening/Speaking-Higher Level

120-90-60 Fluency Activity

Skills: Speaking/Listening

Time: 15 minutes

Level: Intermediate to Advanced

Materials: None

If you want to help your students speak more quickly and fluently, this is the perfect ESL speaking activity for you. Give your students a topic that they know a lot about. For example: good or bad points about their school, university, or hometown. I often give half the students one topic and the other half another just to make it a bit more interesting to listen to. Give your students 3-5 minutes to prepare, depending on their level. But, emphasize that they should just write one or two words for each point, and not full sentences because it is actually a speaking activity and not a writing one.

Then, with a partner, the first student has to give their speech and talk continuously for two minutes, while their partner listens. I use an online stopwatch so that the students can see the clock count down. Then, I give the students another two minutes and they switch roles.

After that, the students have to find a new partner and the activity repeats, except they have to include ALL the same information as before, just in 90 seconds. Then, switch again, with 60 more seconds. One way that you can help your students make the transition to less time is by giving them 30 seconds between rounds to think about how to say something more concisely, go over in their head the part of their speech where they had to slow down for some reason or to think about where they could use conjunctions.

You could give an example of something like this: "I like watching The Simpsons. It's funny. It's interesting. My mother, father, brother and I watch while we're eating dinner almost every night of the week" --->"I like watching The Simpsons because it's funny and interesting. I watch with my family almost every night while eating dinner. "

For lower level students, you can adjust the times to make them shorter and easier because talking for two minutes can be quite difficult.

Emphasize that students must include all of the key information even though they have less time to say it. Speak more quickly or more concisely!

Teaching Tips:

It can be really difficult to find good speaking activities that are focused on fluency instead of accuracy, but this is an excellent one and I try to use it a couple of times per semester.

Emphasize to your students that they must include all the same information they included the first time, so they'll either have to say things more concisely or speak faster. Present it as a difficult, but attainable challenge that they can achieve. At the end of the second and third rounds, ask your students how much they were able to include as a percentage. If they did well, tell them to pat themselves on the back for achieving something that wasn't easy. A small motivational moment in your class!

Something that you can remind your students of is that spoken speech is more informal than written discourse, particularly in the areas of sentence length and connectors. When we write, things like "however," "although," and "moreover" are common but in spoken speech we mostly just use simple connectors like "and," "but," and "or." Also, in spoken discourse the length of an utterance is much shorter and we don't need to use complicated grammatical constructions.

Procedure:

41

1. Give students a topic and some time to prepare their "speech."

2. Students give their speech to a partner, talking for two minutes without stopping. Switch roles and the second student gives their speech.

3. Students find a new partner and give their speech again, this time in 90 seconds. Switch roles.

4. Students find a new partner and give their speech again, but in 60 seconds. Switch roles.

20 Questions

Skills: Speaking/Listening

Time: 20 minutes

Level: High-Beginner to Advanced

Materials: None

This is a "20 questions" style game based on whatever you're studying such as animals or jobs that is particularly effective for working on yes/no question forms and also logical thinking. If you have higher level students, this works well as a warm-up or icebreaker activity. You can leave it open and allow the students to choose any person, place or thing.

The teacher starts the game by thinking of a secret thing and the students can ask the teacher yes/no questions. Keep track of how many questions are asked and incorrect answers count as a guess too. Students can then play the game in small groups or in pairs, which will significantly increase the student talking time.

Teaching Tips:

It is especially important to do a demonstration of this game because in my experience, it isn't played in many parts of the world. You can also coach students a little bit on what good and bad questions types are, such as a guess right at the start of the game is a terrible and too specific type of question but a general question which eliminates a lot of possible answers is a good one (animals: Does it have 4 legs?", or jobs: "Do I need to go to university to get it?").

This game is easily adaptable to make it much easier or much more difficult. To make it very difficult, just say that the secret word has to be a noun. If you want to make it less difficult, specify either a person, place or thing. Finally, the easiest version is to choose a more specific category such as animals or jobs. If you choose the easiest version, you might want to reduce the number of questions from 20 down to 10. For absolute beginners, it's useful to write some example questions on the board for them to refer to throughout the activity.

This is another one of those absolutely nothing required in the way of preparation or materials games which can be played with a variety of levels and class sizes (from 1-40). Keep it in your bag of tricks to pull out in case of emergency.

Procedure:

1. The teacher chooses a secret thing for the example. Students ask a yes/no question. The teacher answers the question and puts one tick (checkmark) on the board.

2. Students ask more questions and the game continues until the students either guess the secret thing or they reach 20 questions/guesses. If you have a small class, it's easy to monitor the activity to ensure that each student gets to ask a question. If you have a larger class, you can make a rule that once a student has asked one question, they cannot ask another one until five more questions have been asked. If the students guess the secret thing, they win. If they reach 20 questions without guessing, the teacher is the winner.

3. Each guess also counts as one question, in order to prevent random guessing.

4. Students can play the game in partners or small groups of 3-5. Whoever guesses the correct answer gets to choose the next secret thing.

Ask Me About

Skills: Speaking

Time: 10-20 minutes

Level: High-Beginner to Advanced

Materials: Name labels

This is not an activity for students who are very shy. Before class, print sticky name tags with "Ask Me About" and a cheeky prompt. For example: ". . . the first time I got drunk," or ". . . my worst date ever." Have students mingle and ask each other the prompt on their name tags. This is better for adults who know each other a bit and should be used after you've had a few classes together. If you feel that cheeky prompts would offend your students, stick to safer ones such as first jobs, or the best vacation.

Procedure:

1. In advance, print an "Ask Me About" name tag sticker for each student. Each should have a different prompt, such as, ". . . my worst date ever," or ". . . my first job."

2. As students come in to class, give them each a sticker to put on like a name tag.

3. Have students mingle, asking each other the prompts on their tags.

4. You can wrap this up by asking a few students the best story a classmate told them.

Cocktail Party

Skills: Speaking/Listening

Time: 10-20 minutes

Level: Intermediate to Advanced

Materials: None

Small talk is a necessary skill, but can be difficult for non-native speakers, especially those from countries where such conversation is not common. Explain to the students that they are at a cocktail party being thrown by their spouse/partner's company. They must engage in small talk with a group of 3-4 people for 2-3 minutes. You may need to scaffold the activity with common cocktail party conversation: current events, sports, even the weather, if they must. Let them know certain topics are typically NOT appropriate at a cocktail party: political opinions, religious discussions, salary, or any other controversial topics. Additionally, demonstrate how to ask follow-up questions.

The main points of the activity are to practice speaking with relative strangers about inconsequential topics and asking follow-up questions. Wrap up the activity by asking each group what topics they discussed and give feedback.

Teaching Tip:

Depending on the level of your students, when you demonstrate the activity, you may need to bring to their attention that you are making follow-up questions based on your partner's answers. Otherwise, your students may end up asking each other a list of unrelated questions without really listening to the answers.

Procedure:

1. Explain to your class that they will be attending a cocktail party for their spouse/partner's company. Their spouse/partner is called away from them (to answer a call, talk to the boss, whatever), so they must mingle alone.

2. Elicit from students typical topics of cocktail party conversation. Add to the list, as necessary: current events, sports, favorite TV shows (particularly very popular ones that the other guests are likely to be familiar with), etc.

3. Elicit from students topics of conversation which would NOT be appropriate, such as salary, age, religion, etc. If necessary, explain that these topics would be considered too personal or controversial for a cocktail party.

4. Have students stand and begin to mingle.

5. After 2-3 minutes, have students change groups. Time allowing, have them chat in three groups for 2-3 minutes each.

Complaint Desk

Skill: Speaking

Time: 10+ minutes

Level: Intermediate to Advanced

Materials: None

Complaining, apologizing, and customer service vary from country to country, so your students may not know how to complain in English. In this role play, students will take turns complaining to a customer service desk and being the representative dealing with the complaints. You can give them a scenario, including the type of business and reason for the complaint, or you can have them brainstorm their own.

Begin the lesson with some useful vocabulary, such as:

Excuse me,

I'm sorry, but...

Would you mind...?

How can I help?

What exactly is the problem?

I'm terribly/so sorry (to hear that.)

To make up for this...

Then, divide your students into pairs. If you are not giving them a scenario, give them 2-3 minutes to brainstorm a time when they had a customer service complaint. You may want to make some suggestions, such as defective merchandise, a disappointing meal, or an incorrect bill. Have the pairs then take turns being the customer and being the employee.

Teaching Tip:

The higher the level of the class, you may want to encourage your students to use a bit more creativity: try to negotiate a lower bill, or (as customer service) give reasons to deny their request, for example.

Procedure:

1. Begin class with an introduction on complaining and apologizing in English and useful vocabulary for making a complaint to customer service.

2. Divide students into pairs. Give them a scenario, or 2-3 minutes to brainstorm their own.

3. Have students take turns being the customer and the customer service representative.

Drill, Baby Drill

Skill: Speaking

Time: 15+ minutes

Level: Intermediate to Advanced

Materials: None

This is a debate topic which may be controversial, depending on where you are teaching, but it is something most people have an opinion about. Divide your class into two teams: environmentalists and oilmen.

Give them the following scenario: oil has been found in your region, but in an area which has not been developed and many people enjoy visiting due to its unspoiled beauty. The proposed project to extract the oil would bring jobs and money to the area, but would spoil the beauty of the area and interfere with the habitat of local wildlife. The oilmen are holding a town hall meeting to address the concerns of the environmentalists who want the area to be protected from any development. So, each of the environmentalists will pose a concern or make a demand, and the oilmen must address their concerns and negotiate with them.

Give the two teams several minutes to discuss their position and try to anticipate the opposition's points in order to be ready to rebut them. When they are ready, or time is up, have them begin. The environmentalists will take turns asking a question or stating a concern. The oilmen must listen and respond in a way that satisfies the environmentalist and furthers the project agenda.

Teaching Tips:

Before class, arrange the desks so one side of the classroom is facing the other. The environmentalists can then face the oilmen. If this isn't possible, have the students stand to speak.

If the students say they don't know much about environmental issues or they don't know how to respond as a business person, talk a bit about how politicians speak. That should be familiar to them.

Procedure:

1. Before class, arrange the desks so one side of the classroom is facing the other.

2. Divide the class into two groups: environmentalists and oilmen.

3. Give the class the scenario (above) and several minutes for each group to discuss their position and try to anticipate the opposition's points in order to be ready to rebut them.

4. Have the environmentalists take turns asking a question or stating a concern.

Group Therapy

Skills: Speaking/Listening

Time: 10-15 minutes

Level: High-Beginner to Advanced

Materials Required: None

In the style of an AA meeting, students sit in a circle if possible and introduce themselves, "My name is _____, and I'm _____." Instead of finishing with ". . . and I'm an alcoholic," finish with a problem they have learning English, such as using articles correctly or conjugating verbs. They should then solicit tips and tricks from their classmates. The teacher should begin by modeling and could give an actual problem they have as a language student. For example, "My name is Jennifer, and I'm never sure how formal or polite to be when speaking Korean to someone I don't know well. Does anyone have any advice for me?"

Teaching Tip:

This is a great first day activity, because it is a not-very-sneaky way to get an idea of what areas of language the students perceive to be more difficult, which you can use to inform your lesson planning for the semester.

Procedure:

1. Before class, arrange the desks in a circle, if possible. If the class is very large, divide students into several large groups.

2. Begin by telling your students that everyone has trouble learning languages, and even those who speak several languages fluently have difficulty with some aspect of any language they learn.

3. Introduce the lesson as "therapy" for them to get counseling for their troubles.

4. Begin with your own example of a problem you have with a foreign language you speak. For example, "My name is Jennifer, and I'm never sure how formal or polite to be when speaking Korean to someone I don't know well. Does anyone have any advice for me?"

5. Go around the circle and give each student a turn to introduce themselves, "My name is _____, and I'm _____." Instead of finishing with ". . . and I'm an alcoholic," finish with a problem they have learning English, such as using articles correctly or conjugating verbs. They should then solicit tips and tricks from their classmates.

Just a Minute

Skills: Speaking

Time: 5-10 minutes

Level: Intermediate to Advanced

Materials: Whiteboard, timer

This is a very simple activity that you can use as a fast warm-up at the beginning of class in order to get your students talking. Write a bunch of general categories on the board such as jobs, hobbies, dreams, movies, food, etc. Put the students into groups of 4 and they can number themselves 1-2-3-4. Then, ask one of the students to throw a paper airplane at the board and whatever word it gets closest to is the topic for the first student. All the number ones must talk about that topic for one minute without stopping and if they stop or have a long pause, they've lost the challenge. You can adjust the time limit to be higher or lower depending on the level of students (beginner = 30 seconds, advanced = 2 minutes). Erase the first speaking round word from the board and continue the activity with the remaining three students except that they have different topics. It's helpful if the teacher does an example speech first with a topic that the students choose.

Teaching Tip:

For higher level students, you can require that their teammates listen carefully and each of them has to ask the speaker an *interesting* follow-up question or two.

Procedure:

1. The teacher writes topics on the whiteboard (teacher-supplied, or elicited from students).

2. Put students into groups of 4. They number themselves 1-2-3-4.

3. The teacher does an example speech with a topic that students choose.

4. One student throws a paper airplane at the whiteboard. The topic closest to where it hits is the first one.

5. Student one has to talk about that topic for a minute without stopping. The goal is to have minimal pauses and to never stop talking. (Optional: the other three students each ask a follow-up question).

6. Erase the first speaking round word. Another student throws the paper airplane and finds another topic. The number two students talk for a minute. Continue with the third and fourth rounds' students.

Man on the Street

Skills: Speaking/Listening

Time: 10-15+ minutes

Level: High-Beginner to Advanced

Materials: Laminated question cards

In this activity, each student takes a turn as the reporter, asking a current events question from a card, and the group members answer as a man on the street. Begin with a discussion of the news and man on the street interviews, and/or prep a few clips of such interviews (you might include a funny one or two, such as "Jaywalking with Jay Leno"), or clips from ELLLO (www.elllo.org) which are non-native speakers. Divide students into small groups and give each member of the group a different question card—the groups can have the same pool of cards.

Procedure:

1. In advance, prepare question cards with one current events question on each card. Laminate them, if you want to use them with more than one class. Optionally, also prepare a few clips of man on the street interviews to show a few examples to students.

2. Begin class with a discussion of the news, specifically, man on the street interviews.

3. Explain to the class that they will take turns being a reporter and the man on the street.

4. Divide students into groups of 4-5 and give each group enough question cards for each student to have a different question.

5. If you want this to be a short activity, have each reporter choose a different man on the street, so each group member asks and answers one question each.

6. If you want to extend the activity, have a group discussion after about the different opinions on current events held by the class members.

Me, Too!

Skills: Speaking/Listening

Time: 5-10 minutes

Level: High-Beginner to Advanced

Materials: None

This is a simple activity to uncover what your students have in common with one another. If possible, arrange the seats in a circle, so everyone can see each other. Begin by sharing a fact about yourself that you don't think is unique or unusual. For example, "I like to hike in my free time." Any students in the class who also enjoy hiking should stand (or raise their hands) and say, "Me, too!" Go around the circle and have each student share one fact about themselves. You could extend the activity by keeping track of numbers and noting which facts are common to the most number of students.

Teaching Tips:

You may need to remind them that these are not unusual facts; these should be things they expect to have in common with at least one other person.

Procedure:

1. If possible, arrange the seats in a circle.

2. Begin by sharing a fact about yourself that you don't think is unique or unusual. For example, "I like to hike in my free time."

3. Ask any students in the class who also enjoy hiking to stand (or raise their hands) and say, "Me, too!"

4. Go around the circle and have each student share one fact about themselves.

5. You could extend the activity by keeping track of numbers and noting which facts are common to the most number of students.

Never Have I Ever

Skills: Speaking/Listening

Time: 10-20 minutes

Level: Intermediate to Advanced

Materials: None

This is a classic party game that you can play in your ESL speaking classes as well. The way it works is that students think of a few things that they haven't done but that they think others in the class have. For example, maybe someone hasn't been to Japan or China but most of the people in the class probably have. Or, perhaps someone has never tried Indian or Vietnamese food. If you have higher level classes, no thinking time is really necessary, but with intermediate students, you might have to give them a few minutes before you start the activity so that they can prepare. You could also elicit a few possible categories such as food, travel, hobbies, free time, etc. if you feel this activity will challenge your students too much when open-ended.

The first student starts with one of their statements, saying, "Never have I ever _____."
The other students listen and if they have done it, they get a point. I usually get students to
keep track of points themselves by writing a tick on their paper or in their notebook. If you
have a small class, you can appoint a captain to do this on the board. You go around the
room until everyone has said at least one statement (for big classes) or a couple of them
(smaller classes) and then tally up the final points. Whoever has the most points is the
"winner" and the person who has had the most interesting life so far! If you have a large class,
it's best to divide students up into groups of 7-10.

Teaching Tips:

This game is quite difficult to explain, even to people who speak English as their first
language so doing a demonstration with multiple examples is vital.

Procedure:

1. Give students time to prepare 2-3 statements; the amount of time depends on the level of
your students. They need to think of things that they've never done, but which they think their
classmates have.

2. The first student says one of their statements. If someone else has done it, they put up
their hand to signify this and they get one point. I usually have students keep track of the
points themselves or appoint a captain to do this.

3. The next person can say their statement and you follow the same procedure, until
everyone has said at least one statement. You can also continue until you've done two or
three rounds, depending on your class size.

4. The person with the most points has had the most interesting life.

Relative Clause Speaking Activity

Skills: Speaking/Listening

Time: 15-25 minutes

Level: Intermediate to Advanced

Materials: Who/what papers (one per group)

Interesting and fun activities or games using relative clauses are not that easy to come by (I've looked!) but this is a good one. I think you'll find your students really enjoy it, and that they're able to use the target grammar quite easily and naturally.

Make a list of things or people, cut them up into little pieces and put them in an envelope (here's my very Korea-centric who/what list). Put the students in groups of four and the first person has to choose a paper at random and keep it secret. Then, they give hints about it, preferably using relative clauses or reduced relative clauses.

For example, if they chose Barrack Obama, they could say things like:

This is a man who's from the USA.

I'm sure he's someone everyone knows.

He has a lot of power which he uses to influence the whole world.

The other three people on the team get to guess who it is and whoever guesses it correctly keeps the paper, gets one point and then is the next person who chooses a random paper and gives hints. In order to avoid endless incorrect guesses, I make a rule that if you make an incorrect guess, you are "out" of that round unless all the other people also have incorrect guesses, in which case it starts over and everyone has one more chance.

Teaching Tips:

I recommend using a somewhat country specific list for wherever you are teaching. I've found that many of my students lack the general knowledge that I think they should have. Maybe it's a culture thing, or maybe it's the age gap but whatever the case, choose many famous people from wherever you're living.

You could challenge your higher level students to use different kinds of relative clauses throughout the game, such as "who," "that," and reduced relative clauses.

Procedure:

1. Prepare a list or pictures of famous people or things.

2. Put students in small groups.

3. The first student must secretly choose one person or thing and give hints, preferably using relative clauses.

4. The rest of the group can guess, but if a student makes an incorrect guess, that person is "out" until the next round unless everyone is also incorrect and then everyone gets another chance.

5. The person who guesses correctly gets one point and a chance to pick the next person or thing.

6. The person with the most points at the end of the allotted time is the winner.

Story Picture Cards Sequencing

Skills: Speaking/Listening

Time: 15+ minutes

Level: Intermediate to Advanced

Materials: Laminated cards which have a sequence of pictures, one per student plus your own

This is an activity better suited to higher level students. In advance, prepare individual pictures which tell a story when put together. Give each student one picture. Without showing one another their pictures, students must discuss the images in order to determine the correct sequence of images which tells a story. When they think they have the correct order, everyone reveals their pictures to see if they are correct.

Teaching Tips:

If the class is very large, have two or even three different sets of pictures, each telling a different story. Clearly mark each set, so students know who they should be working with. This is intended to be a mingling activity, but it could be done in groups while sitting. Make sure the pictures have elements which lend themselves to easier sequencing, such as a clock, the sun/moon, and activities usually done at a certain time, such as eating, commuting, and working.

The books Zoom and Re-Zoom by Istvan Banyai are perfect for this activity, if you can get your hands on a copy. Just be sure to use a sequence of pages in order.

Procedure:

1. In advance, prepare a series of pictures which tell a story when put in order.

2. Tell students they must discuss their pictures without revealing them to each other, in order to determine the correct sequence of the images.

3. When the students all think they have the correct order, have them reveal their pictures to one another to see if they are correct. The teacher can check answers with the class if necessary.

The Refugee

Skill: Speaking

Time: 10+ minutes

Level: Intermediate to Advanced

Materials: None

Optional Materials: newspaper articles or photos of the event

This speaking activity may hit too close to home, so use with caution. It should get your students talking, though! Recently, a Syrian refugee, Osama Abdul Mohsen, was trying to illegally cross a border when a journalist, Petra Laszlo, tripped him. Divide your students into pairs or small groups and have them discuss:

1. Journalists are supposed to report events, not interfere. Should she have been fired for her actions?

2. Should refugees be allowed free access across borders? If not, how should it be controlled?

3. What are some valid reasons for restricting refugees' entry into a country? For NOT restricting entry?

You can end the activity by inviting a few pairs/groups to summarize their opinions on one or more points.

Teaching Tips:

You may want to refresh your students' memory of the event. Links change, so the names of the journalist and refugee are included above.

A less controversial discussion about this event could focus on the refugee being injured, the journalist losing her job, and/or the journalist suing the refugee.

Procedure:

1. Ask your students if they remember the story of the Hungarian journalist tripping the Syrian refugee. If not, review it briefly, show them a photo, and/or have them read a short newspaper article about it.

2. Divide students into pairs or small groups to discuss the above questions.

3. Have a few pairs or groups share their opinions at the end.

Tell Me More

Skills: Speaking

Time: 5-20 minutes

Level: High Beginner to Intermediate

Materials: Topic prompts, phone/voice recorder

This is a test preparation activity for standardized speaking tests. The TOEIC requires test takers to speak on 11 questions for varying lengths of time, while the TOEFL has six questions. Sometimes, preparation time is given but other times it is not. One barrier for many students is that they simply cannot keep talking, even about a familiar topic. In this activity, you will give your students a prompt and record them speaking, so you can record how long they can speak and how much relevant detail they can give.

Consider for example, the question, "How often do you read the newspaper?" If the answer given is, "Never," the student will get a minimum score because the answer is relevant (as in, he/she answered the question), but the student did not provide any detail. There are many ways this answer can be expanded:

"I never read the newspaper because I am too busy. Anyway, I can hear about important events on the radio as I drive to work."

"I never read the newspaper because I can find out all of the news online or by watching the news on TV."

"I never read the newspaper because I know if something interesting or important happens, I will read about it on Facebook."

You can see two things have been accomplished in this example: a reason and a detail have been added to the answer. Obviously, the longer the time limit, the more detail(s) should be given.

To do this activity, give your student a prompt and record their answer. This will give you the exact length of the student's response and you will be able to review the response to determine specific areas which need improvement. By frequently practicing, the student will become accustomed to the format of the response and can focus on the content of their answers.

Teaching Tips:

Use the materials available from the testing company for the relevant test for this activity.

If you do this with a large class, you may want to have them record their answers and upload them to YouTube or email them to you for homework.

Procedure:

1. In advance, prepare speaking prompts from the relevant test materials.

2. Choose a prompt and have your students work individually to prepare an answer.

3. Record the answer or assign for homework, if the class is large. The completed videos can be uploaded to YouTube or emailed to you.

4. Review the answer with the student for length and completeness of response.

5. Repeat this activity frequently if your students are preparing for a standardized test.

Test Prep: Describing a Photo

Skills: Speaking

Time: 30-40 minutes

Level: Intermediate to Advanced

Materials: Prepared images and accompanying vocabulary, timer (phone, kitchen timer, etc.)

Optional Materials: Recording device

Some standardized tests of English ability have a speaking task that evaluates how well the test taker can describe a picture. The image may or may not be accompanied by vocabulary the test taker must use in his/her description. Therefore, for this activity you should prepare several images and vocabulary, such as a noun and a preposition or adverb.

Depending on the level of the class, you may want to begin with some useful language, such as:

at the top/bottom

on the left/right

in the corner/middle

"I think/It looks like _____ (is happening.)"

After you have gone over the useful phrases, divide the class into pairs. Have Student A show Student B a picture and ask him/her what is happening. Set the timer for one minute. Encourage the students to describe it in as much detail as possible. Instruct Student A to elicit further elaboration from Student B, if necessary, until it becomes habit to keep talking for the entire allotted time. Depending on the image, you may want to include hints for Student A to refer to:

"How is the weather?"

"What else do you see?"

"What do you think they are doing?"

"How do you think that person is feeling?"

Have the students switch roles. You should have a different image for Student A to describe.

Teaching Tips:

Remind the students to speak in present continuous when describing the image. ("The sun is shining. The man is looking at the woman as they walk across the beach. It looks like they are happy.")

If your students have voice recorders or phones, record their responses. This will help them track their progress as well as how long they speak each time.

You can extend the activity into general speaking by having a discussion related to one or more of the photos.

Procedure:

1. In advance, prepare several photos for your student to describe to their partner.

2. Review some useful phrases (see examples above).

3. Show a photo to your student and ask him/her to describe it to you.

4. As needed, encourage your student to continue describing the photo.

Test Prep: Reading Aloud Fluently

Skills: Speaking/Reading

Time: 30-40 minutes

Level: Intermediate to Advanced

Materials: Prepared texts

Optional Materials: Recording device

Some standardized tests of English ability have a speaking task that evaluates how fluently the test taker can read a text aloud. To prepare your students for this, choose several short passages for them to read aloud. During class, first model reading the passage aloud and then have your students read it to a partner several times. Walk around the class to monitor and give each student specific pointers after each reading. For example, if his/her intonation or stress needs improvement, mark the text to show which syllables to stress or where the intonation should rise or fall. If your students have voice recorders or phones, have them record your reading as well as his/her final one for review and practice before your next lesson.

Teaching Tip:

I like to use Breaking News English (www.breakingnewsenglish.com) for this activity because there are a number of activities for each story, so you can easily build an entire lesson around one or two passages.

Procedure:

1. In advance, prepare several short passages for your students to read aloud to you.

2. First, model reading the passage aloud, then have your student read it to a partner several times.

3. Monitor, and give specific pointers after each reading.

4. If your students have voice recorders or phones, have them record your reading as well as his/her final one for them to review and practice before your next lesson.

Test Prep Speaking Activity: 5Ws and H

Skills: Speaking

Time: 30-40 minutes

Level: Intermediate to Advanced

Materials: Prepared speaking prompts, timer (phone, kitchen timer, etc.)

Optional Materials: Recording device

The speaking part of a standardized test of English ability has some similarities with the written essay portion: the test taker is asked to speak with minimal or no preparation time about a topic for a specified length of time. However, speaking tests have other elements as well. For example, some tests have speaking prompts focusing on personal experiences. Some common prompts include:

Describe a person who has had a great influence on you.

What is your happiest childhood memory? Why?

Describe a place you like to visit.

To get full marks, test takers need to give a full answer. To do this, have your students think like journalists: 5Ws and H. To use the above example prompt of an influential person, your students should tell who the person is and how the person influenced him/her. Your students should elaborate by including when and where they met. He/she can emphasize how long they have known each other, why the person was influential, and what specific qualities the person has that impressed the student.

When you think your class is ready, divide them into pairs (Student A and Student B), provide a prompt and set the timer to give them one minute to prepare. When the timer goes off, reset the timer for two minutes and instruct Student A to begin speaking. You may want to record your students' answers, or have them record themselves for the two of you to review and to track their progress.

Procedure:

1. In advance, prepare several speaking prompts for your class to answer.

2. You may want to have an example prompt to model fully answering a question.

3. Whether you model the activity or not, point out that each student will need to expand his/her answer to fill the time. Keeping the 5W and H questions in mind will help him/her remember to include a variety of details.

4. Divide the class into pairs. Give each student a prompt and set the timer for one minute to allow him/her to prepare a response.

5. When the timer goes off, reset it for two minutes and have student A begin speaking. Switch roles and student B can speak.

6. Your students can record their answers if they have a phone or voice recorder.

Test Prep: Speaking to Essay Writing

Skills: Writing/Speaking

Time: 40-60 minutes

Level: Intermediate to Advanced

Materials: Prepared writing prompts, timer (phone, kitchen timer, etc.)

If your students are planning to take a standardized test of English ability, they will need to prepare for the timed essay. The essay intimidates many students, but as long as they practice the expected format with the main categories of prompts (choose a side, explain or describe, and compare advantages and disadvantages), they don't need to be worried. One way to ease your students into essay writing is by using the prompt as a guided speaking activity to help them brainstorm and fully develop some ideas and opinions.

Once your students have a good idea on where they stand, they can put pen to paper. I also remind my students that there is no lie detector: if they have an opinion based on one strong reason, but the opposite opinion has numerous weaker reasons, then they should defend the easier position. You can start by introducing some important language such as linking words and phrases and opinion words and phrases.

Some examples of these are:

In my opinion,

On the other hand,

I think/feel/believe _____.

Some people think/feel/believe _____, but I disagree.

I'm convinced/sure/certain/positive _____.

Some would say/argue _____, but to me. . .

Once you have gone over these, give the class a prompt. Have them work in pairs. (You may want to give each pair two prompts or have them work on the same one.) Ask them to answer the question with one sentence. Then, ask their partner why or ask for more detail. For an opinion prompt, try to get everyone to give three or four reasons, and then have them explain or give examples to back up those reasons. The more reasons the better because, once your students start writing, they can focus on the ones that provide the best examples. Finally, have everyone ask their partners about the opposing opinion. Why do some people have that opinion? For choose-a-side prompts, addressing the opposing position is a good topic for the third body paragraph.

Once everyone has talked through their essay, it is time to write. Check the time limit for the test your students (or the majority) plan to take (but most are 30 minutes.) Start the timer and let the class write. You can collect the essays to use as the basis of the next lesson.

Procedure:

1. In advance, prepare a writing prompt of the style used in standardized tests (choose a side, explain or describe, and compare advantages and disadvantages) and a timer.

2. Start by introducing some important language such as linking words and phrases and opinion words and phrases. Some examples of these are listed above.

3. Give the class a prompt. Have them work in pairs. (You may want to give each pair two

prompts or have them work on the same one.)

4. Instruct them to each answer the question with one sentence. Then, ask their partner why or ask for more detail.

5. Once each student has given several reasons and examples, have them ask their partner about the opposing opinion.

6. Start the timer and have the class write the essay within the allotted time.

7. Save the essays to use the next lesson.

The Hot Seat

Skills: Speaking/Listening

Time: 3-4 minutes/student

Level: High-Beginner to Advanced

Materials: None

This is a great activity if you have a small class of no more than 10 students. Each student has to think of one interesting thing about themselves that they want to share with the class. My examples are that I have an identical twin and that my mom is also one (it's really true!), or that I've been to more than 50 countries. Then one by one, students have a chance to sit in the "hot-seat." They say their interesting statement and the class has to quickly ask five follow-up questions. The best thing about this activity is that there are usually a lot more questions that students want to ask and they'll follow up during the breaks or after class.

Procedure:

1. Each student thinks of one interesting thing about themselves.

2. The first student comes to the front of the class, sits in the "hot-seat," and says their interesting statement.

3. The class has to quickly ask them five follow-up questions, to which the student answers,

and then the student goes to sit back down in their regular seat.

4. The next student comes up and the procedure is repeated until all students have been in the "hot-seat."

The Student Becomes the Teacher

Skills: Speaking/Listening

Time: 40-60 minutes

Level: Intermediate to Advanced

Materials: None

Have each student prepare a brief lesson introducing a hobby or interest of theirs. For example, if they enjoy football, they could explain the basic rules. If they insist their only interest is playing computer games, have them introduce their favorite game and explain how it is played. Remind them that they will be explaining their topic to an absolute beginner so they should assume that the other students in the class have no prior knowledge about their topic.

Teaching Tips:

This is not a first-day activity because you need to have an idea of their level and what, if any, scaffolding will be required.

Procedure:

1. In advance, have students prepare a three-minute lesson introducing their hobby or interest. If your class is large or very low level, reduce the time to two minutes.

2. Plan to give each student time to answer questions about their hobby.

3. Depending on the level, you may need to scaffold with a short how-to reading passage, to give them an example of how instructions should be given. As always, model the activity with your own three-minute lesson about your own hobby or interest.

Listening/Speaking-Lower Level

Board Games

Skills: Reading/Speaking

Time: 25-40 minutes

Level: Beginner to Advanced

Materials: Board game sheet and token for each student (a coin or eraser)

Board Games often come in the "teacher's resource book" that goes along with your textbook and if this is the case, you're in luck because no prep will be required but you'll have a solid activity that your students will probably love and it has the added bonus of being extremely student-centered. However, don't worry if there isn't a pre-made game in the textbook because it's easier than you might think to make your own. It will only take 5-10 minutes once you get a bit of experience doing it.

Use questions based on the grammar and/or vocabulary that you've been studying during the previous classes. Have some fun squares, such as, "Switch positions with the person on your right" or, "Go back 5 spaces." The style I typically use is a question of some kind where the student has to speak one or two sentences in response to it. The other students in the group listen for incorrect answers, in which case the student has to move back the number that they "rolled." You can use dice (which gets loud), two coins (2 heads = 5, 1 head + 1 tail = 3, 2 tails = 1), or a number sheet where students close their eyes and move their pen to choose a number.

Check out this blog post (www.eslspeaking.org/board-games-for-esl-students) for more details about board games and an example one that you can use in your classes.

Teaching Tips:

Board games have their own lexical set and it may be the first time many of your students have ever played a board game in English so it's useful to do some pre-teaching.

Before you play, you can teach them some key phrases and encourage them to speak only English (it's your turn, go ahead, your roll, pass the dice, let's ask the teacher, etc.).

Dice are my least favorite way to "roll" because they fall off the desk, roll around the room and they can also be very loud. Using coins or a paper sheet with a pen is much more controlled.

If students disagree about whether an answer is correct or incorrect, you can make a joke and tell them not to fight but just to ask you to be the referee. You should think carefully about your game though and make most of the questions easy enough so that there are obvious correct answers. If not, your class time will be very stressful if you have a big class and many groups demanding your attention at the same time.

Before I give the winner of each group a little prize, I'll often make them answer one or two final questions, which I usually take from the game board. It's a good way to review correct vocabulary and/or grammar use with the class in case any group has been off-base but you didn't catch it. A key component of learning language is hearing it and using it again, and again, and again. Help your students do this in class by doing quick reviews together at the end of activities.

Procedure:

1. Hand out the "game boards" as well as dice or coins to groups of 3-5 students. Have each student provide their own token—it can be an eraser, a key or a small piece of paper.

2. The students can do rock-scissor-paper to see who goes first. The first student uses the dice or coins to find the number of spaces they will move ahead. That student answers the question and if correct, they stay on that space but if incorrect, they move back the number of spaces that they rolled.

3. The next student rolls the dice and answers a question and so on.

4. The game continues until one student reaches the final square on the game.

Bucket Lists

Skills: Speaking/Listening

Time: 10-15 minutes

Level: Beginner to Advanced

Materials: None

Optional Materials: Example bucket list poster or PPT

Give students about five minutes to create a list of three things they want to do, see, or accomplish before they die. Have them partner up to discuss for 2-3 minutes, then change partners.

Procedure:

1. Begin by asking students if they have heard the term "bucket list." Then, show them your example, or simply tell them three things you want to do, see, or accomplish before you die.

2. Give students about five minutes to create their own bucket lists.

3. Divide students into partners to share their bucket lists, then have them change partners. Encourage the students to ask each other some follow-up questions about the list.

Charades with Speaking

Skills: Speaking

Time: 20-30 minutes

Level: Beginner to Advanced

Materials: Whiteboard

You can use this activity to review whatever vocabulary you're teaching (verbs work especially well). Write down some words or phrases that can be easily acted out on small pieces of paper and put them in an envelope.

Divide the class into two teams. The first team sends one person (the captain) up to the front and he/she has to act out and describe in English as many things as possible in two minutes. Alternatively, you can have each team member rotate through the captain role during a single 3-4 minute round. The first person describes the first word and after his/her team guesses it, then he/she can go to the back of the line and the next person comes up. Then, the next team will go. You can do as many rounds as you want with different captains.

Teaching Tips:

To add even more fun, if there is a team that is behind by a lot of points you can have a double and then a triple bonus round to give them some hope that they can catch up and maybe even win.

Procedure:

1. Prepare some words or phrases beforehand, based on whatever you're teaching.

2. Divide the class into two teams and each team can choose its first captain.

3. Team A sends its captain to the front and he/she randomly chooses a paper and must describe and act it out.

4. Team A must then guess what the captain is describing. When the team guesses correctly, the captain takes another word and the game continues. Alternatively, you can have the students rotate the captain role amongst themselves during the course of a single round. In this case, make the round a bit longer—maybe four minutes instead of two.

5. Each round is 2-4 minutes and each team tries to get as many words as possible.

6. The other teams goes next and uses different words.

7. You can play as many rounds as you want, but make sure you have different captains for each one so everyone gets a chance to describe the words.

Conversation Starters

Skills: Speaking/Listening

Time: 10 minutes

Level: Beginner

Materials: None

Students often struggle with how to start a conversation and this is an activity you can use to help them. It's particularly useful for beginners but it's also possible for advanced level students if you give the students a particular context relevant to them such as "at the water cooler" (business small talk) or "at the drink table" (party small-talk).

The way it works is that you write the beginning of a conversation on the PowerPoint or whiteboard. For example,

A: "How was your weekend?"

B: "It was _____. I _____."

Or,

A: "What did you do last night?"

B: "I _____."

Or,

A: "Anything interesting happening with you lately?"

B: "Not really, I've just been _____."

Put the student into pairs and they have to engage in a short conversation for about a minute using the starter. If you have adults, you can ring a bell after one minute is up and then they have to quickly find someone else that they haven't talked to yet and start the conversation again. If you have teenagers, it can get a little chaotic to do it that way so I recommend forming two opposing lines. One line stays stationary while the other line moves one person down the line for each round.

Teaching Tips:

An important sub-skill that our students need to be proficient at is initiating a conversation. However, it can sometimes be a bit of a difficult thing even for English native speakers so it's really useful to provide our students with opportunities to practice it and also to give them a few set phrases they can keep in their English "tool-kits." It can be useful to do this activity at regular intervals (every month perhaps) and use different starters each time.

Procedure:

1. Think of a conversation starter. Put it on the PowerPoint or whiteboard.

2. Have students find a partner, either in a line or by themselves.

3. Students have a one minute conversation using the starter.

4. Ring a bell and students have to find a new partner, either by mingling or moving one space down the line to face a new partner.

5. Students have another short one minute conversation. Repeat as many times as desired.

Describing Something Guessing Game

Skills: Speaking/Listening/Reading

Time: 5-10 minutes

Level: Beginner to Intermediate

Materials: Handout or PowerPoint with approximately 20 pictures

This is a simple warm-up activity that you can use to generate some interest in a topic for intermediate or advanced students or it can also be used as a quick review of the last lesson's contents. For beginners, it's best to play after you've taught them the necessary language to make the sentences instead of as a warm-up at the beginning of class.

Make up a handout or PowerPoint with pictures of around 20 famous people. Give some hints, such as, "He's American," "He's a sport player," and, "He plays golf." By this time the students will have guessed Tiger Woods. You then cross Tiger Woods off their list or delete it from the PowerPoint. Turn it over to the students and they will take turns describing the people to each other.

You can play in pairs, small groups or with the whole class. This activity works for almost any topic (animals/food/clothes, etc.) and is good for teenagers or adults.

Teaching Tips:

A sub-skill that you could focus on using this activity is hedging, which is when we are not sure about something and use language to indicate that. For example, "Maybe it's _____," "It might be _____," "Is it _____?" "It could be _____. "

I emphasize that students should speak in full sentences when they are giving hints to their partners. Simply saying things like, "Man, American, golf" is really not useful for helping students improve their English skills beyond the most basic beginners and even then it's questionable. It's useful to put some example sentences on the board such as "She/He has _____ (hair/eyes)." "She/He is from _____." "She/He is a _____ (job)."

As a general rule, the more that you can get your students speaking in full sentences, the better off they'll be in terms of language learning. It's far easier to let your students just say one or two words, but they're not actually pushing themselves to incorporate grammar constructions into their speech in a meaningful way. But, of course don't forget that spoken discourse has much shorter sentences than more formal written work, so don't push students to use more complicated grammatical constructions when doing a simple speaking activity like this.

You can put in a few fun pictures to make it more interesting. For example, I'll always include a picture of myself in a situation where it might not look like me because I had a different hairstyle or was wearing glasses. Or, I'll put in a picture of my twin sister (I really do have a twin!) You can also add a picture of a student in the class or another teacher at your school that the students would know.

Procedure:

1. Prepare pictures of famous people on a handout or in a PowerPoint. PowerPoint is easier and better, but check how it will look on the big screen first before using it in class. Sometimes low-quality pictures can look terrible when made bigger. Also, be careful if you

print out the pictures because you'll often need a really high quality printer in order to make the pictures easily recognizable.

2. Do one example with the students so they get an idea of how to play.

3. Put the students into partners or small groups. The first student chooses someone secretly and describes him/her to his/her partner, who must guess the person, using hedging if they are unsure about the answer. You can also allow your students to ask some "W/H" questions to their partner if they wish.

4. The students switch roles and continue until the time is up. In order to avoid frustration, I usually make a limit for each picture of two minutes because there might be one that the guesser really just doesn't know.

Deserted Island

Skills: Speaking/Listening

Time: 5-10 minutes

Level: Beginner to Advanced

Materials: None

Deserted Island is an excellent way to uncover what things are most important to students. Tell students that there is a terrible storm and their ship is sinking, but thankfully, they can bring three objects with them. It doesn't need to be realistic or necessary for survival, just something that they want to have with them during their time on the island. Encourage creativity and imagination. Then, have students share their answers with the class (if under ten students), or in small groups (in larger classes), and give a reason why they'd bring each item.

Procedure:

1. Tell students that they are on a ship and it's sinking. Thankfully, there is an island nearby that is already well-stocked with everything they'll need for survival.

74

2. Each student has to choose three things that they'd like to have with them during their time on the island. It doesn't need to be realistic or necessary for survival.

3. Students share their answers and why they chose each item with the class (if under ten students), or in small groups (in larger classes).

Draw a Picture, but Someone Else is Talking

Skills: Speaking/Listening

Time: 10-15 minutes

Level: Beginner to Intermediate

Materials: Blank paper

This is a fun way to practice body parts or descriptive words (big, small, long, etc.) and I guarantee that everyone will be laughing throughout this activity. The students sit back to back and one person is the "talker" while the other one is the "drawer." The person talking describes something that they're looking at to their partner (a face, a body, a city, a monster) and that person draws what they hear. The results are usually hilarious and fun to show to the rest of the class!

Teaching Tips:

Some useful functional language that you can practice with this activity is asking for clarification. You can pre-teach some language surrounding the topic, such as:

How _____ (long, tall, etc.)?

What do you mean?

I didn't understand, could you say it again?

What did you say? I couldn't hear you.

This activity can get quite loud so it's best to ask students to spread out in the classroom, if possible.

If you teach absolute beginners this is also a great activity, but you might have to do it in a more teacher-centered way. For example, the students could describe a picture to you that you draw on the board, or you could describe something to them and they all draw their own versions of it.

Procedure:

1. Two students sit back to back but close enough to talk to each other.

2. Give student A a picture of some kind, based on whatever you are studying. I usually put something up on the PowerPoint and have the drawer sit with their back towards the screen.

3. Student A describes the picture to student B who must draw it, without looking at the original picture. Student B can ask some questions to student A to clarify if necessary.

4. Compare the original picture with the drawing and laugh a lot!

English Central

Skills: Listening/Speaking

Time: 10-15 minutes

Level: Beginner to Advanced

Materials: Internet connection

English Central (www.englishcentral.com/videos) is YouTube for language learners. There is premium content and functionality, but you can enjoy many features for free. YouTube, of course, has subtitles on some videos, but English Central takes it to the next level. First, the videos are intended for use with students, so they have been curated and organized by level, topic and/or language skill. Each video is segmented for easy replay of a chunk of speech. Students can also click on a single word to hear it pronounced slowly and learn the definition.

Pronunciation is one activity you can use English Central for with your students. Have them listen to a clip and repeat. You can pause after each phrase or sentence and repeat as needed.

Begin by playing the entire clip once or twice. Then, replay the clip, bit by bit, for the students to repeat. Each clip is a short story, so you can also watch and discuss and/or summarize it.

Teaching Tips:

If your students have difficulty with a particular word, you can click on that word and it will be played in isolation. If the students have trouble with a sound, rather than a word, there is a pronunciation section that focuses on phonemes.

Procedure:

1. In advance, make sure you will have an Internet connection.

2. Either select a video in advance or let your students choose one. There are "courses" that are sets of related videos, that you can work through in a series.

3. Play the clip once or twice first so the students can hear the entire thing.

4. Play one segment (sentence or phrase) at a time and have the students repeat, trying to copy the pronunciation.

5. End by watching the entire clip one more time and discussing and/or summarizing.

"Find Someone Who _____" Bingo

Skills: Speaking/Listening/Writing

Time: 10-15 minutes

Level: Beginner to Advanced

Materials: Blank "Bingo" grids or blank paper (optional PowerPoint or white board and marker)

This is a good icebreaker to help students get to know one another or to practice asking and answering questions about likes/dislikes, future plans, hobbies, etc. If I have my own classroom, I keep a stack of blank grids handy, but if I'm moving from class to class, I tend to have students use their notebooks.

To save time, I prepare a PowerPoint with possible items to complete the Bingo grid, such as a list of hobbies, jobs, places, etc.—whatever topics you want to include. If I'm using this as an icebreaker, I may list hobbies, musical instruments, and popular films or games so students may learn that one student plays the cello and another studied science in university. If we are practicing future plans, this list might include jobs, places, types of housing, etc. and students will then practice saying things like, "I want to be a manager," "I want to buy a bigger apartment" or, "I want to buy a BMW."

Rather than have a Bingo caller, students must circulate around the class and ask each other questions to mark out items on their grid. For example, if the topic is jobs, they could ask, "What do you do?" I have them write the other student's name in the grid, rather than simply cross it out. So, if a student says, "Doctor," they will write that student's name in that block. Before you begin, give them a target of one line, etc. to get Bingo.

Teaching Tips:

Rather than make a PowerPoint, you could simply write the items on the board. If you want to give students more autonomy, simply give them a topic and have them brainstorm. You should have more items than will fit on the grid, but you can use 3X3 or 4X4 grids if you want to make the activity go more quickly.

I encourage students to move around by only allowing each name to be used once per board in a large class. If the class is quite small, two to three times on a 5x5 grid may be necessary. The goal is to have students practicing the target language, rather than standing with one person and saying, "Do you like apples? Oranges? Bananas? Pears? Melons? Bingo!"

Procedure:

1. Optional: prepare Bingo grid cards and a PowerPoint with questions before class. Otherwise, have students use notebook paper. Tell them what size grid to draw: 3x3, 4x4, or 5x5.

2. Have students fill in their grid with items from the PPT or whiteboard, or create their own,

according to a given topic, such as hobbies or likes/dislikes.

3. Have students mingle and ask questions to match students to their grid spaces. For example, student A asks, "Do you like apples?" If student B answers, "Yes, I do," student A writes their name in the "apples" box and moves to the next student.

4. The first student to get a Bingo by finding different students to complete their grid is the winner.

Find Something in Common

Skills: Speaking/Listening

Time: 10-15 minutes

Level: High-Beginner to Intermediate

Materials: None

This activity is an excellent way for everyone to get to know each other. The students stand up with a piece of paper and pencil in their hand. They have to talk to everyone in the class to try to find something in common (they are both from Seoul, or they both know how to play the piano). Once they find this thing in common, they write it down along with the person's name. Keep going until most of the students have talked to everyone.

Teaching Tips:

This is a great activity for students to practice the sub-skill of initiating a conversation, which is something that many of them find quite difficult. You could coach your students before the activity starts and give them a few phrases or conversation starters to keep in their head if they get stuck. However, since this game is mostly for higher level students, I wouldn't write them on the board because students will be referring back to them throughout the activity when they are actually capable of remembering a few phrases in their head and can recall them easily.

Many students struggle with speaking because it happens in real time. Unlike in writing, where we can plan first and then produce later, in speaking, planning and production overlap and often happen at the same time. If our students focus too much on planning, fluency can suffer. If they focus too much on production, accuracy can suffer. In this activity, fluency is far more important than accuracy because the students are having short, small-talk type conversations. I tell my students not too worry too much about choosing the perfect vocabulary word, or exact grammar constructions, but instead just focus on communicating quickly, in a way that is "good enough."

Tell your students that while it is okay to have short conversations about the thing they have in common, the goal of the activity is to try to talk to most of the people in the class, so they need to keep moving and talking to new people. I recommend to my students that they try to spend only 1-2 minutes talking with each person.

Procedure:

1. Students stand up with a pencil and paper in their hands.

2. They talk to another student and try to find something they have in common by asking some questions. Questions that work really well are ones like, "Have you ever _____ (lived abroad)?", "Are you _____ (an only child)?" or, "Do you _____ (have a brother)?"

3. Once they find something in common, they write that down, along with the person's name.

4. Then, they find a new partner and continue until they've talked to everybody in the class or the time is up.

Four Corners

Skills: Listening

Time: 5 minutes

Level: Beginner to Intermediate

Materials: None

This is an opinion poll activity. Students start in the middle of the classroom. Designate each corner as: strongly agree, strongly disagree, no opinion, don't know about the topic. (You can give other options, if you would rather they choose a definite opinion.) Give them a controversial statement, or at least something most will have an opinion about. Have them move to the corner that matches their opinion. Once everyone has moved, give them another statement. Continue for five minutes, or 5-10 statements.

Variation: Only have two opinions: strongly agree/disagree or love/hate.

Teaching Tip:

Prepare your classroom in advance, so there is room to move around the class and room to gather in the corners. If your classroom is too small, try the variation with only two opinions, so students only need to gather on one side or the other.

Procedure:

1. In advance, clear enough space in each corner of the room for students to gather.

2. Designate each corner as: strongly agree/strongly disagree/no opinion/don't know about the topic. Alternatively, you could divide the classroom in half: agree or disagree.

3. Give students a controversial statement. Prepare 5-10 statements in advance, focusing on recent news items, or other topics your students are likely to have an opinion about.

4. Have students move to the corner/side which matches their opinion.

5. When everyone is in a corner, give them a new statement and have them move again.

6. Continue for about 5 minutes or 5-10 statements.

Hidden Object Pictures

Skill: Speaking

Time: 10-15+ minutes

Level: Beginner to Advanced

Materials: Worksheet, crayons or markers

You may remember hidden object pictures from your childhood. While they may seem a bit juvenile, coloring is currently quite trendy, and your students may get a kick out of this. If you have some Photoshop skills, you could alter an "adult" coloring page to fit this activity.

If you haven't done this before, it is a drawing with a number of objects "hidden" in the picture. Obviously, it is best suited to teaching nouns. Students should work in pairs or small groups, discussing the picture as they look for the list of objects. In any case, you don't want your students to sit silently for an entire class period coloring.

Teaching Tips:

If you want to make sure each person has a fairly equal amount of speaking practice, give each member of the group a part of the list. This will force students to ask each other what objects are on the other lists.

If you decide to have students color, then you don't need a full set of crayons or markers for each student. Put two complete sets in baskets or cups for each table to share.

Procedure:

1. In advance, prepare a hidden object picture worksheet (there are many available for free online) and, optionally, bring sufficient crayons or markers for the class.

2. Begin with a brief review of the vocabulary related to the hidden items.

3. Divide students into groups of 2-4 and have them work together to find the hidden images.

4. Finish by having students show their pictures and naming the images they have found. You can extend the task by having students describe the main image, as well.

Making Videos

Skills: Speaking
Time: 1-5 hours

Level: Beginner to Advanced

Materials: Smartphone and/or computer

For my conversation classes, I rarely give the students written homework. It doesn't really make sense and it seems far better to me that my students have to practice speaking. Plus, at least in Korea, everybody loves using their Smartphone so this gives my students another excuse to do this.

I base the homework on whatever we're studying. For example, in one of my higher level classes we were talking about good and bad manners, so I had my students choose a specific situation (going to someone's home, at a coffee shop, eating out, etc.) and explain what things you should and shouldn't do. For lower level students, I've done things like telling students to introduce themselves and then giving a few topics that they have to cover such as family, hobbies and hopes for the future.

It's really easy for the students to upload the videos on *YouTube* and then send you the link so you can watch and evaluate them. To make it even more fun for the students, I tell them that they can make the video with someone else if they wish. If it's a person in the same class, the requirements are usually slightly higher (for example, five minutes instead of three). But, they could also do it with anybody outside the class. I've had students get their families, little brothers or sisters, girlfriends or boyfriends, international students they know in their dormitory, and even random people on the street to help them. It's usually really funny and interesting and it's homework that I truly don't mind grading.

You could show the videos in class if you want, but I often don't since there are always lots of students in Korea who are really shy. However, if students know that other students will be watching their videos, motivation is higher and the videos tend to be better quality. Another thing you can do is to have students watch the other videos and comment on them as part of their homework but be careful with this and make sure to provide specific rules for what kinds of comments are allowed if you teach teenagers because they can sometimes be less than kind.

Teaching Tips:

Getting your students to make videos is a particularly effective way to work on functional language or language sub-skills. Some things you could focus on for solo videos include: giving an opinion, offering advice, using more or less formal language depending on the situation, marking the main points of a discourse through emphasis, and verbal cues or transition statements. If there are two or more people, you can focus on the things previously mentioned but could also consider making a request, apologizing, agreeing, disagreeing, asking for an opinion, turn-taking skills, initiating, etc. What you choose to focus on depends on the topic you choose and whether the student is alone or with a partner. For example, in solo speech it can be really useful to focus on something like grammatical accuracy, pronunciation or intonation. However, in a pair your students could work on offering advice, or transition statements.

Even if you're not stellar at using technology, chances are that your students mostly are, especially if they are teenagers or university students so don't let this hinder you. I've found that even the mature students in my classes could figure it out, usually by asking their own teenagers or students (many of them are teachers themselves.) Of course, you should put up your own video on *YouTube* first so you at least have a basic idea of the process. If students are having particular problems, I recommend instructing them to Google it in their own language because the question has surely been answered already.

I never give additional points or take away points for things like poor sound or lighting quality as long as I can see and hear them. I instead focus on English use, since it's an English class and not a video making or editing one. That said, if a student uses their creative powers and goes above and beyond what the other students have done, I'll usually give them a bonus point or two and even ask them if I could show their video in class to the other students.

Some students worry about privacy issues so I always mention that I'll grade the videos very quickly (within a day) and as soon as they get an email from me with my comment, they can delete the video. Another option is to have students send you the video itself by email or upload it to a shared *Google Drive* or *DropBox* account.

Procedure:

1. Decide on the criteria for the video: alone/partner/group, length, topic, etc.

2. Explain the criteria very clearly to your students and either have them work on it in class or for homework.

3. Students can upload the video to *YouTube* and then send the link to the teacher.

4. There are three options for watching the videos:

A. The teacher watches them and writes comments for the students.

B. You watch them in class, with an optional Q&A time.

C. Students watch each other's videos outside of class and leave a comment. I do not recommend this option for teenagers due to the bullying factor. However, it works quite well with university students and adults.

Only 1 Question

Skills: Listening/Speaking

Time: 10-20 minutes

Level: Beginner to Intermediate

Materials: Pen, paper

Students have to think of one single question about a certain topic. For example, if you're studying about holidays, they could use any of the following:

"What's your least favorite holiday?"

"What did you do last _____?"

"What do you think about Valentine's Day?"

There are many possibilities but I usually make a couple rules that it must be interesting and also that it can't be a yes/no question. Once students have done this, they ask at least 10 people their question and quickly record their answers with 1 or 2 words. After the time is up, they tabulate the answers and can quickly report to a small group what they found out about the topic. You can ask each small group to share the most interesting thing they learned with the entire class.

Procedure:

1. Give students a topic and have each student make one *interesting* question about it. Give them examples of interesting versus boring questions.

2. Each student talks to 10+ students, using the same question. They quickly write down answers with 1-2 words.

3. Students tabulate the results and report them to a small group of 4-6 people (or the entire class if fewer than 10 students).

Password

Skills: Speaking/Listening

Time: 10-20 minutes

Level: Beginner to Intermediate

Materials: List of words, whiteboard

This activity helps students review vocabulary and practice an important skill: describing something they don't know the word for. Divide students into two groups. The groups will alternate sending a team member to stand at the front of the class with his/her back to the board. Write a word over the person's head, so the team mates can see it but the student cannot. The team must give that person hints until he/she guesses the word or time runs out (20-30 seconds). The team with the most points wins.

Variation:

Have one team's turn last until they run out of time (2-4 minutes) and then switch. This gives an advantage for correctly guessing more quickly. Pause the clock between answers so a new team member can take the hot seat.

Procedure:

1. In advance, prepare a list of words. These can be vocabulary taught in class or just words you expect your students to know.

2. Divide class into two groups.

3. Have groups alternate sending a member to the front of the class, or give each group a time limit of 2-4 minutes and rotate team members as soon as one guesses a word, until time is up.

4. Write a word on the whiteboard over that person's head, so his/her team can see it, but the student cannot.

5. That student's team must give the person hints until he/she guesses the word or time runs out (20-30 seconds).

6. The team with the most points at the end of all the rounds is the winner.

Phone Show and Tell

Skills: Speaking/Listening

Time: 10-15 minutes

Level: Beginner to Advanced

Materials: Students' phones, optional PPT image of a photo from your phone

In small groups, each person chooses one image on their phone to share with the group. They should show the image and discuss what's happening and why they chose to share it.

Teaching Tip:

An easy way to quickly change groups is to number students, for example, 1 to 4. When you change groups, tell all 1's to get together, 2's together and so on. Be sure to show each new group where to sit. If you have ten groups, you can simply divide the new groups in half.

Procedure:

1. Optional: in advance, prepare a PPT of an image from your phone.

2. Divide students into groups of 3-5 and ensure that any students who don't have a phone are divided evenly among the groups.

3. Show the PPT and tell students that it is a picture from your phone. Discuss the picture; tell what is happening and why you chose to share that particular picture.

4. Instruct them to take out their own phones and give them 2-3 minutes to choose a photo to share with their group.

5. If you want to extend the activity, you can have students change groups and repeat the activity, either with the same image or after choosing a new one to share.

Poster Project Group Presentation

Skills: Speaking/Listening

Time: 5-10 hours preparation, 1 hour presentation time (depending on class size)

Level: Beginner to Advanced

Materials: Large poster paper

If you want to do some task-based learning in your class, this is an excellent one to do. Put your students in groups of 2-4 and assign a topic or theme. If you're studying about food, you could tell your students to choose a popular food in their country. If your class is about current events or social issues, each group could choose one of those.

Then, students will have to make a poster with some pictures and a minimal amount of text. Emphasize the minimal text because if you don't, many of the posters will be filled with a large amount of text that is impossible to read. It's a good idea to draw a model poster on the white board and draw big pictures with examples of writing size and content. You can point these things out as you give instructions.

Once the poster is complete (give class time, or for homework), the group will make a presentation about the topic. I emphasize that each group member must talk for an equal amount of time and that they must memorize their presentation and cannot read from a paper. Finally, I ask them to prepare a few quiz questions (3-5) for their classmates to test and see if they were listening! You can also include some Q & A time if your class is outgoing and they won't be too shy to do this.

Teaching Tips:

This is an excellent activity to use if you want to focus on stress and intonation with your students. You can show them how to use these things to emphasize the key points, signal a transition or signal what is old and what is new information.

You could also consider introducing some markers that are present in more formal kinds of spoken discourse such as this one. For example, there are standard ways to introduce a topic (Today, I'm going to talk about _____), develop an idea (I'll talk about three main points related to this), transition into another idea (Now that you've heard about A, I'd like to talk about B), or conclude a presentation (Remember the most important points are _____.)

While not a lot of preparation is required for this since your students are doing most of the work, you need to be really clear in your head about what your expectations are and you also need to convey this really clearly to your students. If you don't, you're likely to be disappointed in the results, but it will be your fault and not the students'. It can be helpful to prepare a list of "Top 10 Dos and Don'ts" on a handout or on a class website or *Facebook* group.

It is extremely important to get students to memorize their speeches and to ensure this, you can allocate a large amount of points (20-30%) to it if the assignment is graded. If you don't, the presentation will likely be terrible and will often consist of simply reading from a PowerPoint or a piece of paper. I do however tell my students to bring their script up to the front with them and they can look one time per person without any penalty in case they truly forget what they need to say.

Procedure:

1. Put students into groups and assign a topic.

2. Give explicit instructions about what is required of them regarding the poster and the presentation.

3. Have students prepare the poster and the presentation, either in class or for homework.

4. Students do their presentation in front of the class.

5. The students ask their classmates some quiz questions based on what they talked about.

6. Question and answer time (optional).

Puzzle Finder

Skills: Speaking/Listening

Time: 10-15 minutes

Level: Beginner to Intermediate

Materials: Puzzle pieces (from an actual puzzle or a cut and laminated image)

The objects of this activity are both teamwork (to create the puzzle) and a review of common vocabulary, such as colors, shapes, and common objects. Before class, you should either prepare a puzzle with enough pieces for each student to have one or two each, or print an image which you cut into the correct number of pieces and laminate. The former is easier, but the latter gives you much more flexibility and you can cut the pieces as large as you like.

In order for students to put the puzzle together correctly, they will need to be able to describe their piece to others as they mingle looking for adjacent pieces, as well as listen to others' descriptions.

Teaching Tips:

If you are using a ready-made puzzle, a child's puzzle will have the right combination of large size and a low number of pieces. If you choose your own image, you can print the pieces even larger, making it easier to work together.

To make the task more challenging, have students describe their pieces to one another, rather than show them. To make the task less challenging, have two puzzles (fewer edgeless pieces) or use an image with obvious elements, for example, a picture of a park, rather than a Picasso.

Procedure:

1. In advance, either get a puzzle with enough pieces for each student to have one or two (so, no 500 piece monster puzzles) or print an image (A3 or larger), cut it into the right number of pieces, and laminate it.

2. Give each student a puzzle piece or two, and instruct them to work together to complete the puzzle.

3. According to the level of the students, allow them to show each other the pieces as they work or require them to describe the shape of their piece and the image fragment.

QR Code Hunt

Skills: Speaking/Listening

Time: 15-60 minutes

Level: Beginner to Intermediate

Materials: Internet access, printer, tape/Blu-tack, student phones with QR code reader apps installed

This activity requires a bit more prep than others, but (as of writing) the novelty factor is high enough to draw some students in who might otherwise be too cool for school. Classtools.net makes it easy to put together a QR code hunt, so don't worry if you haven't used QR codes before—if you can type, you can do this activity.

Teaching Tip:

You can go in a few different directions with this activity, and a pub quiz is a light-hearted way to get students talking, just make sure the questions aren't so obscure that your students spend the entire class Googling the answers!

Procedure:

1. In advance, write your questions in a Word document. These can be discussion questions, trivia questions (pub quiz), or you can pre-test student levels, particularly if you are teaching a subject class.

2. Go to http://www.classtools.net/QR/ and copy and paste.

3. Create the QR codes and print.

4. Post the printouts in various places around the class, or better yet, a larger area.

5. Before dividing students into groups, make sure at least one member of each group has a QR code reader on their phone. If not, give them a minute to download an app—there are plenty of them and most adult students will already have one.

6. Divide students into groups of 3-4 and give them a time limit to find and answer all of the questions.

7. Particularly if you plan to assess student levels, as an option you can have students write the questions they find, and their answers.

8. Wrap up the class with a group discussion of the answers.

Quiz Show Review Game

Skills: Speaking/Listening

Time: 30-45 minutes

Level: Beginner to Intermediate

Materials: PowerPoint chart, or white board and questions

This is a "Jeopardy" style quiz game, which is useful for teenagers all the way up to adults. It works especially well as a review game before a test. Although most teachers spend a lot of time making this game by using PowerPoint, it really isn't necessary and you can simply write up the grid on the whiteboard before class starts in less than a minute. It should only take you 5-10 minutes to prepare the questions if you're very familiar with the material so it really is a low-prep game.

Make up categories based on whatever you have been studying. For example: "vocab, can/can't, movies, body, etc." Think of questions that range from easy ($100) to difficult ($500). Put the students in groups of 3-4 and they have to pick their category and question. The students can pick whatever they want, but the key is that if they get it correct, they get the points. If wrong, they get minus that number. I put in a few +/- $500/$1000 and choose your own wager (up to $1000) to make it more interesting and give the lower level teams a chance to catch up.

There are a few different ways that you can get students to answer questions such as being the first entire team to put their hands up, or hit a buzzer but that can get pretty chaotic. Instead, I do this activity in a more controlled fashion with each team choosing questions in order, one at a time.

One very fun category that I like to include is "random," where I ask any sort of question that we didn't specifically talk about in class. It's more like a general knowledge or trivia category. You could also include a category called, "All about _____" where you ask the students questions about yourself. Only include those things that you've mentioned in class before and observant students will be able to answer.

Teachings Tips:

Something I do to make it more interesting for the other teams who are not answering the question is tell the students that some of the questions from the game are actual questions on the exam that they're usually doing the next week. I don't think I've ever had so many students paying such close attention to anything before! And of course, put in a few of the game questions on the test to reward those who were listening closely.

If you want to make this game more student-centered and also practice writing and questions forms, you can get the students to make the questions. Put the students into groups of 3-4 and give them the general categories. Then, for each category, they have to submit one easy, one medium and one difficult question. Compile their questions and play the game in the next class you have together. A team might be lucky and get their own question, but it shouldn't happen too often.

Procedure:

1. Make a list of review questions. This depends on the number of categories but 25 works well (5x5).

2. Make sure each team gets asked an equal number of questions.

3. Put students into teams of 3-6 and do rock-scissor-paper to see who goes first.

4. The first team chooses a category and a price. Ask them that question. If correct, they get the points and you can eliminate that question from your board. If incorrect, they lose those points and that question remains in play so that another team can answer it.

5. The next team chooses a question. Follow the same procedure as above.

6. Continue the game until most or all of the questions are gone and all the teams have had a chance to answer an equal number of questions.

Scrabble

Skill: Writing

Time: 10-15 minutes

Level: Beginner to Advanced

Materials: Oversized wall-mounted board, or one board per table and a set of letters

Your students will likely be familiar with Scrabble, either the board game or similar apps. It's a great way to get students to recall vocabulary and use correct spelling. It's a bit labor intensive to create the board(s), but I get several years of use out of a wall-mounted board.

To make a wall-mounted board, I use a large (big enough for letters to be seen across the classroom) piece of felt. Thin quilt batting is not as durable, but may be easier to come by. The Velcro on the back of the letters will pull bits of it off, but I still can get enough use out of a board to make it a viable option. I use an actual board as a guide for number of squares and arrangement of "special" squares, but I add in a few more than in the standard game. Wikipedia has the official list of number of letters and point value, which I use as well.

I make the letter cards about the size of my hand so that the words can be read across the classroom. I laminate them (of course!) and stick a square of "pointy" Velcro on the back. Since the board is felt or batting, the Velcro sticks right on.

If the class is lower-level, I have the students work in pairs or threes. If the class is quite large, I use table-top game boards. You can splurge and pay for real boards, but I just use A3 paper. I make a top board and bottom board, print them, cut off the border at the join, laminate them, and tape them together. You will need a set of letters of the appropriate size, but you don't need Velcro.

Teaching Tips:

To increase the challenge, you can limit them to words they have studied, for example, as a semester review. However, the game itself is likely to be challenging enough. In fact, I usually give a bonus of one point per letter, and sometimes a further bonus for 6+ letter words, to encourage longer words.

Procedure:

1. In advance, prepare one wall-mounted board with letter cards with Velcro on the back, or enough game boards and letter sets for each table to have one. (I use Wikipedia for the game board layout and letter point values and numbers.)
2. Depending on class size and level, have students work as individuals, pairs, or threes. (A large class playing as individuals on a wall-mounted board will create a lot of downtime.)
3. You may want to give bonuses for longer words. If necessary, start a new word in a corner of the board or add a long word of your own if there is a large number of 3-4 letter words.

Show and Tell

Skills: Speaking/Listening

Time: 1-2 minutes per student (no questions). 4-6 minutes per student (with questions)

Level: Beginner to Intermediate

Materials: None

This is a classic activity from way back in elementary school but it can work well in your ESL classes too. Tell students a few days before the "show and tell" class that they need to bring an object from home that is meaningful to them. If it's something really big (a piano) or something that doesn't transport easily (a cat), then they can email you a picture to put up on the screen instead. Students give a short presentation, talking about the item and why it's meaningful to them. The audience can ask a few follow-up questions. In order to make the question time go more smoothly with shy classes, you can put students into teams of 4-6 and each team has to ask one question. You could also award points or a reward to the 3 or 4 students who ask the most thoughtful questions.

Teaching Tips:

This activity is an excellent way to get your students doing presentations in a low pressure way. If they have something familiar to hold on to, they'll feel less nervous than standing in front of the class with nothing. In addition, everybody likes talking about themselves!

Instead of doing this activity in a single class, you could do it over the course of a semester with one or two students going at the beginning or end of class; you can assign specific days to each student.

Procedure:

1. Tell students to bring a meaningful object from home, or send a picture if bringing the object isn't practical.

2. Students introduce the object in a short presentation of 1-2 minutes, depending on the level.

3. The other students listen and can ask some follow-up questions.

Splice Video Introduction

Skills: Speaking/Listening

Time: 45+ minutes

Level: Beginner to Advanced

Materials: iPhones, iPads, and/or iPod Touches, Splice app, Internet access, large monitor

Splice is a very basic, easy to use video creation app, which unfortunately does not have an Android version, as of writing. Like the QR Code Hunt activity, this is using a bit of technology to make something old new again; in this case, tired old self-introductions.

Begin class by showing a Splice video introducing yourself to the class. The video should be about 30 seconds long. Then, have students work in small groups of 3-5 taking turns filming one another's brief self-introductions of around 30 seconds each. If you are worried about their technological proficiency, there are *YouTube* tutorials which show just how easy it is to use this app. When everyone in the group has been filmed, the videos are stitched together and emailed to the teacher to show on the big screen for the class.

Teaching Tips:

If possible, provide several devices yourself with the app already loaded to save time. If this is not a first day activity, find out in advance which students have iPhones or iPads and ask them to come with the app already downloaded.

If your class is very large, even 30 second clips will add up, particularly since they need to be filmed, combined, and then shown to the class. So, a shorter alternative might be necessary, such as having students work in groups of 5-6 to create a 20-second group cheer that they create to introduce their group.

Procedure:

1. In advance, prepare a 30-second video using Splice to introduce yourself to the class.

2. Divide students into groups of 3-5 and have them take turns filming one another's brief self-introductions of around 30 seconds each. Larger groups will need more time but fewer devices.

3. Optionally, show a YouTube tutorial, if your students seem unsure of how to use the app.

4. When all students in a group have finished filming, the segments should be stitched together and emailed to the teacher.

5. When all the videos have been emailed and downloaded, show them to the class on the big screen.

Steal the Eraser

Skills: Listening/Speaking

Time: 10-15 minutes

Level: Beginner to Intermediate

Materials: 2 chairs, a table or desk, eraser

Divide the students into two teams. Have two desks at the front of the class, facing each other with an eraser in the middle of the two desks. One student from each team comes and sits in the hot seat. Rotate through the class so that all the students get a chance to play at least once. You then ask a question of some sort, which you should prepare beforehand (one round = one question/2 students. Two rounds = one question/student. Include a few extras for a "bonus" round). The first person that grabs the eraser can try to answer the question. A helpful rule is that the student can take the eraser whenever they want, but the teacher stops talking as soon as the eraser is touched. The student then has ten seconds to answer as you count down on your fingers. If correct, they get one point. If not, the other player gets a chance to answer the question after you repeat the full question one more time.

To make it even more exciting or if one team is behind by a lot of points, have a "Bonus Round," where the teams pick their best three players and each question is worth three points.

Teaching Tips:

Emphasize that the first student to touch the eraser must take it in order to prevent any chaos. I also require students to keep their fingers on the edge of their desks when I begin the question. It's really important to stop talking the instant one student touches the eraser. If not, students will just grab the eraser and wait for you to finish the question, which is really unfair. It's best to use questions that have very well-defined answers so you don't have to make any judgement calls because half the class will be unhappy with you no matter what decision you make.

Procedure:

1. Prepare two desks facing each at the front of the class, with an eraser in the middle.

2. Divide students into two teams.

3. Each team sends up one person to the front and they sit at the desks. I don't let students choose the person for each round but simply make them go in the order that they are sitting.

4. The teacher asks a question (prepare the list beforehand), but stops speaking once the eraser is touched. Alternatively, you can have each team appoint a captain who takes turns reading the prepared list of questions in order to increase student talking time.

5. The first player to touch the eraser must answer the question within ten seconds. Count down the time on your fingers.

6. If correct, he/she gets one point and the next two people come up to the front for another question.

7. If incorrect, the teacher reads the question (in full) one more time and the opposing player gets a chance to answer the question within ten seconds.

8. If correct, they get one point. If incorrect, both players sit down and the next pair comes up. You can share the correct answer with the class before saying a new question.

9. Continue until all students have had a chance to play at least once.

Student Engineers

Skills: Speaking/Listening

Time: 5-10 minutes

Level: Beginner to Advanced

Materials: Disposable cups and pipe cleaners/uncooked spaghetti/wooden skewers

Optional Materials: Ticking time bomb sound effect

This is a popular activity and is easy to adjust according to what materials you have on hand or can acquire easily. Divide the class into groups of 3-4 and give each group the same assortment of items. Easy ones to prepare are disposable cups and pipe cleaners/uncooked spaghetti/skewers. Give them a building task, such as building the tallest tower.

Teaching Tips:

A ticking time bomb sound effect is really fun, because students will start racing to build faster and inevitably some will destroy what they have built. Yes, I amuse myself in mean ways sometimes.

You could just have them build a house of cards, but having them incorporate a variety of materials requires more creativity.

I've given one example of a tower made of cups and skewers, because those are cheap, easy to find, and not much of a hassle to transport, but you can literally give them any assortment of random objects. If you really want to tap into their creativity and develop team-work, don't give them a set end product; have them decide in their groups what they will build then each group can introduce their product to the class.

Procedure:

1. In advance, prepare "building materials" so each group has the same assortment of items. You want them to have plenty of each item, at least 20-30 cups and skewers, for example.

2. Divide the class into groups of 3-4 students and give each group the same assortment of items.

3. Give them a building task, such as building the tallest tower, and a time limit. The shorter the time, the more pressure will be on, and the more fun to watch.

4. When time is up, the group with the tallest tower is the winner.

Talk Show

Skills: Speaking/Listening

Time: 15 minutes

Level: Beginner to Advanced

Materials: None

Optional Materials: Toy microphones, video clip with monitor)

This is a pair work variation of self-introductions. My higher level students tend to find this more fun than the same old self-introductions they do all the time. I set up the front of the class as a talk show set with a desk and chair (for the host) and a chair for the person being interviewed. Then, I divide the students into pairs. Before beginning, I introduce the activity by asking students about talk shows. Most students will be very familiar with the concept. We then discuss what kinds of questions a host might ask.

One pair at a time comes to the front and the two students take turns being the host and the guest. The host is given either a set number of questions to ask or a time limit. After each host's time is up, the teacher can open the floor to "audience" questions.

Teaching Tips:

While introducing the topic, it may be helpful to brainstorm a written list of questions on the white board for them to refer to as needed. However, you will need to remind them that talk show hosts look at the person as they ask questions.

The larger the class, the less time each pair will have to speak in front of the class. So, if your class is very large, limit each pair to 2-3 questions each before switching roles. If you have a large class and a short period, this may not be a feasible activity for even an entire class period.

Procedure:

1. Before class, set up a desk and chair and another chair, similar to the set-up of a talk-show.

2. To demonstrate, show the class a short clip of a popular celebrity being interviewed on a talk show to show the class, or simply talk about talk shows: what kinds of questions are asked, etc.

3. Divide students into pairs: interviewer/host and guest. (They will switch roles.)

4. Have one pair at time come to the front of the class (the audience) and conduct their interviews. The guests are playing themselves—this is a self-introduction.

5. After a set number of questions (about 5) or your time limit, allow questions to be asked by the audience. Then, have the students switch roles.

Tic-Tac-Toe

Skills: Listening/Speaking

Time: 15 minutes

Level: Beginner to Intermediate

Materials: Whiteboard

This is a review game for students to play in small groups. I usually make groups of four and then within the group, there are two opposing teams. Have students make a regular tic-tac-toe board in their notebook or on some scrap paper. Put up a list of review questions in a PowerPoint, or give students a handout. The teams take turns answering the questions and if correct, they get to mark a square on the grid with X or O and the first to get three in a row is the winner. The teacher can act as the referee in case of uncertainty about an answer.

Teaching Tip:

This game isn't fun if your opponent doesn't know how to answer any questions or has never played tic-tac-toe before so in order to prevent this, I put students in teams of two, trying to match a higher level student with a lower level one. Hopefully, at least one of the students will be able to answer questions and has some sort of tic-tac-toe skill. If you know that many students will have a difficult time answering the questions, you can put some answer prompts up on the whiteboard or PowerPoint.

Procedure:

1. Put students in groups of four, two teams of two.

2. Students can make a normal tic-tac-toe board on a piece of paper.

3. Put review questions in a PowerPoint, or give students a handout with them.

4. One person from each team does rock-scissor-paper to determine who will go first.

5. The first team has to answer the first question and if correct, gets to mark the board with either an X or O. The other team answers the next question and gets to mark one spot on the board if correct.

6. The first team to get three Xs or Os in a row is the winner.

7. You can play numerous games and even have the "winners" move up and the "losers" move down like in King's court until you have one final team that is the "King."

Typhoon

Skills: Listening/Speaking

Time: 30 minutes

Level: Beginner to Intermediate

Materials: White board and questions

This is a fun review game that any age group of students will love that requires a little preparation but no materials. Every single time I play it, my students always want to play again and talk about it for the rest of the semester. Draw a grid on the board, marking one row with numbers and one with letters. 5x5 works well for a 30 minute game. Put in two or three of each of the special letters (T/H/V), secretly on your master paper, but not the board. On the board will just be a blank grid.

T = typhoon: lose all your points

H = hurricane: pick 1 team for minus 5 points

V = vacation: get 5 points for free

E = easy question: 1 point

M = medium question: 3 points

D = difficult question: 5 points

Fill in the rest of your grid with these easy, medium and difficult questions. Then depending on how big your class is, make 4-5 teams. They pick a square, (B-6 for example), then you write the letter in the box and ask them the question or reveal the "special square" that corresponds to it. Have a list of easy/medium/hard questions prepared beforehand. If they get the question correct, give them the points and if not, erase the letter in the box and another team can pick that square if they want and get the same question.

Teaching Tips:

If one team is running away with certain victory, you can adjust it on the fly by switching some squares around but don't be obvious about it. For example, if the team who is in the lead gets a vacation or hurricane, you can easily switch it with an easy question. Then later in the game, hopefully one of the last place teams will get the vacation or hurricane instead (remember a hurricane is where that team can choose another team to lose points, therefore reducing the gap).

If you want to make it more fun, you can be kind of dramatic when writing the letter up in the grid on the board. For example, just do the single line-stroke to start off T, H, E, etc. and students will be anxious to know what it is (because the horizontal strokes of each letter are missing). I also often say things, "Ooooohhhh, bad weather is coming." Or, "Hmmmm . . . the sky is getting very dark."

Make sure that all the students get a chance to participate by saying that once a student on a certain team has answered a question, they can't answer again until all the other team members have. However, their teammates can help them by giving some hints if necessary so that the lower level students won't feel embarrassed or like they're letting down their teams.

Procedure:

1. Prepare review questions beforehand, as well as a "grid" with the appropriate letters marked on it (T, H, V, E, M, D).

2. Write the corresponding grid on the whiteboard, but be sure not to reveal the letters. It should just be blank at this point.

3. Put the students into 4-5 teams. They can rock-scissor-paper to decide who goes first. The first team chooses a square and then you reveal which letter it contains. If a special square, perform that action and if a question, ask the appropriate level of question. If the answer is correct, they get the points and that square is finished. If incorrect, nothing happens and that square remains in the game.

4. The next team chooses a square, performs the action, and so on it goes with the next team.

5. Keep track of the total points and continue the game until all squares are revealed.

Used Card Salesman

Skills: Speaking/Listening

Time: 15-20 minutes

Level: Beginner to Advanced

Materials: Playing cards cut into pieces

This is a negotiation activity. In advance, take a deck of playing cards and cut each card into an equal number of pieces (2-4; the more pieces, the longer the game). Mix the cut cards and divide into the number of groups you will have.

Divide the class into groups of 3-5 and give each group their pile of cards. Give them 2-

3 minutes to sort their cards and see how many complete cards they can make with the pieces that they have, and which pieces they need to complete their cards. Once the cards have been sorted, instruct them to complete their missing sets. Give them a time limit of about 10 minutes.

The goal is to have the largest number of completed cards at the end. Students will have to negotiate with other groups, trying to get missing pieces while trying to keep all of the pieces they have. You will soon see which group has the slickest salesmen.

Teaching Tips:

If you want to try this activity with lower level students, begin by reviewing some negotiating language, like trade. You could demonstrate by offering to trade with a student something from your desk for something on their desk.

You may want to even the odds by having an equal mix of pieces, such as 1-2 complete sets, X number of half sets, and Y number of single pieces. Or you may want to stack the deck, so to speak.

Procedure:

1. In advance, prepare a deck of playing cards by cutting each card into 2-4 pieces.
2. In class, tell the students that they must practice their salesmanship on their classmates. Explain that they will receive cut up cards and must try to make sets of complete cards. At the end of the activity, the group with the most sets will win.
3. Divide the class into groups of 3-5 and give each group an equal share of the mixed card pieces.
4. Allow 2-3 minutes to sort the cards, so each group can see which card pieces they have and make note of which pieces they need to complete a set (a set being a complete card).
5. Give students ten minutes to complete their missing sets, but don't give them any further rules. They should consider as a group whether it would be better to work together or split up and approach different groups at once.
6. When time is up, have each group tally how many complete sets they have and how many

single card pieces they still have.

Vocabulary Apples to Apples

Skills: Listening/Speaking

Time: 30+ minutes, including deck-building

Level: Beginner to Advanced

Materials: Paper, pen/pencils, textbooks, scissors

Apples to Apples is a game in which players defend their choice of card played. This version is somewhat different than the actual Apples to Apples game, in order to increase speaking time. Before playing, students need to make two decks of cards using vocabulary words. This is best done at the end of a semester or book, so that there are more words to play with. You may also want to encourage them to brainstorm words they've learned previously.

For deck-building, divide the students into at least two groups: nouns and adjectives. If you have a large class, you may want to further divide them, for example, into person, place and thing groups. The groups should compile as many nouns and adjectives as they can. To keep the two decks easily identifiable, you can use two colors of paper or blank and ruled paper that has been cut into 8-10 pieces.

Collect the cards once the groups have finished creating them and keep the nouns and adjectives separate. Divide the class into groups of 5-8 students and have each group pick a judge. This person will be in charge of the decks of cards and also will have to choose the winner of each round. Each judge should be given an equal share of the two decks.

Have one group help you play a demonstration round in which you are the judge. Deal each group member five noun cards. Turn over one adjective card and have each student choose the noun card in his/her hand that best matches the adjective and give it to you. Read each of their cards and have students explain why their word is the best match. When all students have spoken, announce which card is the winner, and why.

Have the judge in each group deal five noun cards to their groups and turn over/display one adjective card per round. Players must choose the noun card in his/her hand that they feel best matches that adjective and give it to the judge. The judge takes all of the noun cards and shows each card one at a time. Players must defend their card when the judge shows it.

Example:

If the judge draws the word "*big*,: the other students may submit nouns like "*watermelon*," "*elephant*," "*heart*," and "*day*." The students can then defend their choices with a single sentence:

A: A watermelon is a big fruit.

B: An elephant is a big animal.

C: A kind person has a big heart.

D: An important day is a big one.

The students should then be encouraged to keep talking in order to convince the judge that their answer is the best.

When all players have spoken, the judge will decide the winner of that round. Each player will be given one more noun card by the judge. The judge will then give both decks to the winner of the round and that person becomes the new judge. He/she turns over the next adjective card to start the next round. If there are not many cards (vocabulary words) to play with, you may want to mix the discards back in to the live decks.

Teaching Tips:

While you can save a fair bit of class time by preparing the decks yourself, you can sneak in a bit of parts of speech review for students if they have to make the cards themselves. Additionally, as they are compiling the decks, students are also likely to come across words they have forgotten. This gives them a chance to discuss vocabulary with their teammates before the game begins (at which point their teammates will have little incentive to help.)

Procedure:

1. Before class, prepare cards by cutting sheets of colored printer paper into 8-10 pieces. Use two different colors.

2. Divide students into groups to build two decks of cards: nouns and adjectives. Students should use their textbooks and also brainstorm as many words as they can and write one word per card.

3. When the decks are ready, divide the students into groups of 5-8.

4. Divide the two decks equally between the groups and keep the two separate.

5. Have one group come to the front of the class to demonstrate. You will be the judge.

6. Turn over one adjective card. Have your group look at their cards, choose the noun that best matches the adjective, and give it to you.

7. Read each noun card and have the student who gave it to you defend his/her choice (see example above). Choose the best answer and tell the class why.

8. Have groups play rock-scissors-paper to choose the first judge for their group and play one round.

9. After each round, each player is dealt a new noun card, and the winner becomes the new judge (or you can have them rotate in a circle.)

10. Used cards can be mixed back into the decks if there aren't many cards.

Vocabulary Pictionary

Skills: Speaking/Listening

Time: 10-15 minutes

Level: Beginner to Advanced

Materials: Whiteboard, marker, eraser

Optional Materials: Flash cards

This is a great review game with no prep required. Simply divide students into teams and choose which team will go first. That team will choose a representative to go to the whiteboard and he/she will have to draw pictures (I use a pile of flashcards) that their team guesses. The goal is to get as many points as possible in a specified amount of time (two minutes). Then, the next team does the same thing. You can play as many rounds as you wish.

I use this with classes of up to 40 students and it works well as long as no one gets too rowdy. In those large classes, have students sit at tables, rather than individual desks, so that they can work together easily. If you have a large class seated at desks, you should arrange them into groups of 4-8 desks depending on class size. If you have a class of ten or fewer, just divide them into two teams.

Procedure:

1. Divide students into equal teams of 4-8. Have each team choose a representative to draw.

2. Demonstrate by drawing a picture representing a familiar term on the whiteboard and elicit guesses from the students.

3. The team that correctly guesses the word will go first. The other team representatives will play rock-scissors-paper to determine their order.

4. Have the drawer from the first team go to the whiteboard and show him/her a flashcard. He/she has to draw it.

5. As he/she draws, his/her team guesses the correct word. The drawer takes another card and the team continues to guess. Continue until the specified time is up.

6. Continue until each team has had at least one chance to play.

Where Are They Now?

Skills: Speaking/Writing

Time: 10-15 minutes

Level: Beginner to Advanced

Materials: None

This is a post-reading extension activity that can be done orally or in writing. When you finish a novel or story, have the student imagine the main character five or ten years in the future. Where are they? What are they doing? How have the events in the story affected his/her life?

Teaching Tip:

If your student has difficulty, help them with brainstorming. Show him/her how to make a mind map with items such as: relationship, job, hobbies, home, pet, etc. Talk with your student about how his or her own life has changed in the past five or ten years.

Procedure:

1. After reading a story or novel, discuss how the character changed over the course of the story and why.

2. Have your student write or discuss what he/she thinks the character's life is like five or ten years in the future.

Would You Rather

Skills: Speaking/Listening

Time: 5-10 minutes

Level: Beginner to Advanced

Materials: List of questions

"Would You Rather?" is a fun party game. You can buy ready-made decks, but they aren't ESL specific. I make my own cards, but you can just make a list of questions or do this without materials if you can think of choices on the spot. One example is "Would you rather have eyes like a fly, or eyes like a spider?" The student must choose one and explain why. You can also share your answer and have a short discussion about it.

Procedure:

1. In advance, prepare cards with two choices—the weirder, the better. For example: "Would you rather have eyes like a fly, or eyes like a spider?" If you want to do this without cards, simply give the student two choices.

2. Have a 1-2 minute discussion. The student can also ask you a question if they would like.

Picture Quest

Skills: Reading

Time: 20-40 minutes

Level: Beginner to Advanced

Materials: Picture quest sheet and cameras/phones (1 of each per team)

An excellent way for students to get to know each other is to have some fun together in small groups. The picture quest is one of my favorite activities to help students get to know each other on a more personal level through working together in a team. The way it works is that you give each group a list of things that they must take pictures of, in no particular order. You should require that each group use only one camera/phone so they don't split it. Then, the first team to come back with everything correct is the winner. If there are some errors, you can add some total time to the score and find the winner that way. I usually give out some prizes such as a candy bar or notebook to each person on the winning team. It's possible to extend this activity by sharing the pictures with other teams through a class website, or other media platform.

Here's the picture quest that I use in my own classes:

Rules: only 1 camera

The pictures must be taken today

You can't draw something on the board and take a picture

Only 1 picture 1 time (total of 24 different pictures required)

If you make a mistake, the penalty is +6 minutes to your time.

Any order is okay

1. Of someone wearing something green

2. Of something you can recycle

3. Of something **healthy** you can **_eat_**

4. Of someone who works at this university

5. Of something very big

6. Of something that is strange to see at a school

7. Of a flower

8. Of ALL your group members

9. Of a map

10. Of someone smoking

11. Of 3 people together. 1st person = no feet on the ground. 2nd person= 1 foot on the ground, 1 foot **not** on the ground. 3rd person=2 feet on the ground.

12. Of something that is wet

13. Of something that is too hot to touch

14. Of a cat or dog (real!)

15. Of someone in a suit and tie

16. Of a bus

17. Of an insect or bug

18. Of a TV

19. Of something that is dirty

20. Of the best place to eat lunch at our school

21. Of somewhere that is very relaxing

22. Of somewhere that is very stressful

23. Of something that is interesting

24. Of something that is funny

Procedure:

1. Give each group one picture quest paper.

2. Go over the rules together as a class.

3. Give the students 5 minutes to talk together and formulate their plan (no pictures yet though!).

4. Send students out to complete the quest.

5. Check the pictures from each group as they come back. If there are any mistakes, add six minutes to the total time.

6. The team with the lowest time is the winner.

Reading

Concentration

Skills: Reading

Time: 10-15 minutes

Level: Beginner to Intermediate

Materials: Concentration cards

This is a memory game designed to help students remember vocabulary words and definitions. Make up sets of cards with words on half the cards and the matching definition on the other half. A total of 16 cards (8 sets of words and definitions) works well. Make enough cards so that there is one set for each group of four students.

Students mix up the cards and put them face-down on the desk in an organized fashion. The students play rocks-scissors-paper. The first student chooses two cards and places them face up on the desk so that everyone is able to see them. If they make a set, the student keeps the cards (they're removed from the game), gets one point and is able to choose again. If they don't make a set, the student places them face-down in the *same spot* (it's a memory game!) and the game continues with the next student.

Procedure:

1. Make concentration card sets of words and definitions (16 cards per set, one set per four students).

2. Have students mix the cards and place them face down on the desk in an organized manner.

3. The first student chooses two cards and places them face up on the desk. If they make a set, the student keeps the cards and get one point. If they don't make a set, the student places them face down in the same spot and the game continues with the next student who reveals two more cards.

4. The winner is the student with the most points.

Correction Relay

Skill: Reading/Writing

Time: 10+ minutes

Level: High-Beginner to Intermediate

Materials: Worksheet

This is an activity that uses speed and competition to make something old (error correction) new again. Students of all levels should be quite familiar with finding and correcting errors in sentences. By adding a relay aspect, it will (hopefully) make an important but sometimes tedious skill new and more interesting.

To prepare the activity, create a worksheet with 10-15 errors. You can focus your errors on one aspect of vocabulary, such as synonyms and antonyms, or more simply, misuse vocabulary words in sentences. For lower level students, limit the errors to one per sentence. Higher levels can handle multiple errors in one sentence, and you can increase the challenge by having one vocabulary error per sentence and one or more other errors, such as grammar or punctuation mistakes.

The activity itself is straightforward. Students will work in teams of 4-5 to correct the worksheet as quickly as possible. Each student makes one correction and passes the worksheet to the next person who makes the next correction. They continue to pass the worksheet around until it is complete. You can make it easier by allowing students to choose any remaining sentence to correct, or you can require them to work from top to bottom.

Teaching Tips:

To prevent one student from carrying the rest of the team, do not allow other team members to correct another correction. That is, a sentence cannot be corrected by a second student once someone has corrected it. This also prevents more assertive (but not necessarily more able) students from incorrectly correcting others' work.

Also, to keep things moving along you may want to have a time limit for each turn before students must pass the worksheet along.

Procedure:

1. In advance, prepare a worksheet with 10-15 sentences containing vocabulary errors.

2. Divide students into groups of 4-5. If possible, group the desks to facilitate easy passing of the worksheets.

3. Have students take turns making one correction and, passing the worksheet to the next student to make one correction. They continue passing and correcting until the worksheet is complete.

4. When all teams are finished, go over the errors as a class. The team with the most correct sentences wins.

Cosmo Quiz

Skills: Speaking/Listening/Reading

Time: 10-20 minutes

Level: Intermediate to Advanced

Materials: A Cosmo quiz or Cosmo-type quiz

If you are a guy, you may not be familiar with the quiz in each month's edition of *Cosmopolitan* magazine. These generally predict something about your relationship style, finances, etc. In other words, they are quiz-style horoscopes. They are pretty fun to do as a group, because they are not meant to be taken seriously, but can tell you a little something about the quiz-taker.

Prep could not be easier. Simply find a few old issues of Cosmo and copy the quizzes. Some of them are a bit risqué, so decide for yourself if you want to edit them a bit. I've had all-female classes, and kept it a little racy, but all the students were about my age.

In class, begin with a brief discussion of personality quizzes: has anyone ever taken one, etc. Divide students into pairs or small groups of 3-4 and give them one or two quizzes with the results on a different page. Have them read the questions and discuss the answers, keeping track of their answers, if they want. You can wrap up with a survey of results and questions of how students feel about the quizzes. Are they accurate, fun, or a waste of time?

Teaching Tips:

You can find quizzes on their website: http://www.cosmopolitan.com/content/quizzes/, but the questions are given one at a time, so if you can get your hands on print quizzes, it will make your life easier.

If you think they are inappropriate for your class, you can always just make up a quiz in the same Cosmo style: ten multiple choice personality questions with points assigned to each answer. There are usually results for three point ranges.

You can either give everyone one quiz and each group reads and answers the questions together, or you can have students alternate asking and answering. You can extend the activity by having students change partners and taking a different quiz.

Procedure:

1. In advance, gather several different issues of Cosmo magazine and copy the quizzes. You may need to edit the questions or leave some out.

2. Begin class by asking if anyone has ever taken a personality quiz and how they feel about them.

3. Divide students into pairs or small groups of 3-4 and give them one or two quizzes with the results on a separate page.

4. Have them read the questions and discuss the answers, keeping track of their answers, if they want.

5. Optionally, extend the activity by having groups change partners and take a new quiz.

Disappearing Words

Skills: Reading

Time: 10 minutes

Level: Beginner to Intermediate

Materials: Whiteboard

This vocabulary game is an easy way to force students to keep a set of new vocabulary words in their heads, or to review past words. Write down 10-15 words on the whiteboard and give students 1-2 minutes to study them. Then, if you have a big class, ask everyone to close their eyes as you choose one or two words to erase. Students open their eyes and have to tell you what is missing and where it was. If you have a small class, you can choose individual students to close their eyes and then tell you the missing word(s) after you've erased them. You can either write those words in their spots again or add new words to the mix and continue the game.

Procedure:

1. Write down 10-15 vocabulary words on the whiteboard.

2. Have student(s) close their eyes as you erase 1-2 words.

3. Students open their eyes and tell you which words are missing and where they were.

4. You can write those same words back in, or add new words to the mix in those same spots and continue the game.

Extensive Reading Context Clues

Skill: Reading

Time: 10+ minutes

Level: Intermediate to Advanced

Materials: Story or novel

This activity helps students develop their ability to use context clues when reading.

Simply have them write down five words they do not know as they are reading. Have them note the page number and paragraph to easy reference. Once they have finished reading, have them find those words again and write down the sentence it is used in as well as the sentence before and after it.

Once they have written these sentences, have them use the sentences to guess the meaning of each unknown word and write that as well. Finally, have them compare their guess to the dictionary definition. Are they close? If not, was the word used in an ambiguous way, or could they have made better use of context clues?

Teaching Tip:

Once they are familiar with this activity, you may want to relegate it to homework.

Procedure:

1. As an addition to a regular reading activity, have your students make note of five words in the story they do not know.

2. Have them make note of each word, the page number, and the paragraph number and continue reading.

3. Once they have finished reading, have them go back and find those words again and write down the sentence it is used in as well as the sentence before and after it.

4. Then, have them use the sentences to guess the meaning of each unknown word and write that as well.

5. Have them compare their guesses with the dictionary definitions of each word.

Find the Reference

Skills: Reading

Time: 10+ minutes

Level: Beginner to Intermediate

Materials: Newspaper article, pen

This is a noticing activity. In newspaper writing, care is taken to avoid repetitive use of the subject's name. This is the opposite of most ESL material, which makes frequent use of repetition to reinforce language. Your students will read a newspaper article and circle all references to the subject in order to practice recognizing the subject even when various terms are used to reference it. For a completed example of this activity, please see: www.eslspeaking.org/reference.

Teaching Tip:

Use an actual newspaper, rather than a source such as Breaking News English (www.breakingnewsenglish.com), which may alter the text to reduce the use of varied referents.

Procedure:

1. Choose an article from a newspaper that has multiple references to the subject but uses a number of different referents such as, "Jones," "he," "him," "the 39-year-old," "the painter," "the father of two," etc.

2. Have the students read and circle each reference to the subject.

Story Timeline

Skills: Reading/Listening/Speaking

Time: 10-15 minutes

Level: Beginner to Advanced

Materials: None

Optional Materials: Sentence strips of important events in a novel

Extensive reading is an excellent way to build your students' vocabulary quickly, but you and your students probably don't want to spend too much class time reading novels.

What you can do is assign a novel for homework and in each lesson, go over unfamiliar vocabulary or situations as well as any number of extension activities. This is one such activity and it can be done individually or in small groups.

A timeline, or chronology, of important plot events is a useful way to have the class briefly summarize the story chapter by chapter. A timeline will help them keep track of the story while providing practice determining important events. With lower-level students, you may want to scaffold the activity by providing the sentences for the students to order.

Teaching Tips:

If you are providing sentence strips, you can add extra, unimportant plot events and have the students select only the important ones to order.

Penguin has six levels of graded readers that include simplified versions of popular novels and classics.

Procedure:

1. (Optional) In advance, prepare sentence strips describing important events in the plot.

2. Have the students either order the sentence strips you have provided or determine the events on their own. If you are not using sentence strips, you can have the class complete the activity orally or in writing.

Word-Definition Match

Skills: Reading

Time: 5-10 minutes

Level: Beginner to Intermediate

Materials: Cards or worksheet/whiteboard/PowerPoint

Card Version: Print one word or definition per card. You will need one set per student, pair or group. This version is good for pair/small group work and adds a speaking component to the task.

Worksheet/Whiteboard/PowerPoint Version: Create a word bank of current or review vocabulary and a list of definitions for students to draw a line (worksheet) or matching letters and numbers for whiteboard or PowerPoint.

Procedure (Card Version):

1. In advance, prepare cards with one word or definition per card. Print and laminate enough for each student, pair or group to have a set.

2. If you're having students work in pairs or small groups, divide the class accordingly and distribute a full set of cards to each. If students will be working alone, give each student a set of cards.

3. Have students match the words to their definitions as quickly as possible.

Procedure (Worksheet/Whiteboard/PowerPoint Version):

1. Have students match the words and definitions, by drawing a line (worksheet) or matching letters and numbers and writing their answers in their notebooks.

2. Have students trade papers to check.

Writing

Chapter Response

Skills: Speaking/Writing

Time: 10-15 minutes

Level: Beginner to Advanced

Materials: None

Optional Materials: Printed list of questions

Chapter endings make handy stopping points to check your students' comprehension and build a bit of interest to keep up motivation for the next chapter. These questions can be answered orally as part of a book discussion or written in a reader response journal and then discussed in class.

Some questions you can ask include:

What surprised you in this chapter?

What feelings did you have as you read? What made you feel this way?

What words, phrases, or situations in the chapter would like to have explained to you?

Would you recommend this novel to someone else? Why or why not?

How do the events in this story so far relate to your life?

Which character do you most relate to? In what way?

Which character most reminds you of someone in your life? In what way?

What do you hope to learn about (a character) as you continue reading?

What do you think will happen next?

What questions do you have that you hope will be answered in the next chapter?

Procedure:

1. In advance, prepare a printed list of questions about the chapter.

2. Discuss together in class, or have the students write their answers for homework and you can discuss them in the next class.

Character Problems and Solutions

Skills: Speaking/Writing

Time: 10-15 minutes

Level: Beginner to Advanced

Materials: None

This is a post-reading activity to include in a novel study or use with a short story. Choose a problem a character faced in the story. Discuss the problem and how the character solved it. Then, have your students brainstorm other ways the problem could have been dealt with. This is a sneaky grammar lesson. You can teach modals of regret (could/should/would have done/etc.) without getting too personal with your students.

Teaching Tip:

If your students are lower level, you may want to begin with a complete grammar lesson with scaffolded practice, such as worksheets, for the students to get some more focused practice.

Procedure:

1. Choose a problem a character faced in the story.

2. Discuss the problem and how the character solved it.

3. Have your students brainstorm other ways the problem could have been dealt with.

Choose Your Own Adventure Group Writing

Skills: Speaking/Writing

Time: 1+ class periods

Level: High Beginner* to Advanced

Materials: Blank story maps

Optional Materials: Story starters

Choose Your Own Adventure stories are fun to read, and can be fun to write. The group aspect can be helpful for brainstorming story ideas and, of course, many hands make light work. Even the students most resistant to writing will appreciate that ¼ of a story is less work than an entire story. *This activity will work best with Intermediate and above students, but adventurous High Beginners could enjoy creating simple stories.

If your students are unfamiliar with this style of story, you can show them this example: www.halfbakedsoftware.com/quandary/version_2/examples/castaway.htm. If you show this example to students above the High Beginner level, make your expectations clear or you may well end up with just a sentence or two from each student.

To begin the writing activity, divide the class into groups of 4. You can either give your students a scenario which requires a choice to be made, or allow them to brainstorm their story from start to finish. Each student will need a blank story map to plan their writing. Each group should work together to begin their story, then break into pairs to write the second stage, and finally each write one ending. They will need to discuss the options they write about, so they will each have something different.

Some examples of scenarios are:

A. You go to several job interviews and are offered three jobs: one that is high paid, but will require you to work long hours and live away from your family; one that is low paid, but is rewarding and will give you plenty of free time; and one that has no salary, but pays a high commission and allows you to work the hours you choose. Which job do you choose?

B. Your friend falls and breaks a leg while the two of you are hiking. You cannot get a phone signal. Your friend knows how to read a compass and map, but you do not. Do you turn back alone and try to retrace your steps, stay and hope that someone else passes by, or try to carry your friend back?

C. You are on a space ship that has just arrived on a new planet. You don't know what to expect when you open the doors. Do you send one person out to explore alone or stay together? Do you walk out with your weapons ready to fire or with your arms open to show you aren't dangerous?

Each group would need to choose two of the options and break into pairs. Each pair would write about one option and lead to another choice. For example, with Scenario A, the choice could be about taking a promotion which changes the working conditions (for example, the low-paid rewarding job could lead to a raise, but much more paperwork), buying a house, starting their own business, etc. Since the two pairs are following different options already, they do not need to face the same type of choice, unless you want them to. So, one pair may choose between staying at the low-paid job they enjoy or being promoted, even though it wouldn't be as enjoyable and the other pair could choose between buying a fancy house with a big mortgage or paying cash for a small apartment.

When each pair has a new choice to make, each person will choose one option. Working individually now, each person would finish the story by following the option they have chosen. So, there will be one beginning, two middles, and four endings.

Procedure:

1. Begin by asking your students if they are familiar with Choose Your Own Adventure stories. If not, show the example linked above.

2. Divide students into groups of four. Either give them a scenario (several are suggested

above), or have each group brainstorm their own.

3. All four group members will collaborate on the beginning of the story, up to the first point of making a decision.

4. The group will divide into pairs and each pair will collaborate on one option each.

5. When the next option is given, each student will choose one option and write that ending for the story. So, there will be one beginning, two middles, and four endings.

Make a Sentence

Skill: Writing

Time: 5 minutes

Level: Beginner to Intermediate

Materials: None, or worksheet/whiteboard/PowerPoint

To practice current or review vocabulary, have students make 1-5 sentences.

No Materials Version: Have students use their books and choose a given number of words to make sentences.

Whiteboard/PowerPoint Version: Give students a list of words to use all or some of.

Worksheet/PowerPoint Version: Fill-in-the-blank or multiple choice with a word bank.

Procedure:

Begin with a brief oral review of the vocabulary words you want them to work with and elicit from the students what the words mean.

No Prep Version: Have students take out their books and notebooks and tell them a number of sentences to make using those words. For example, "Turn to page 53, and choose three vocabulary words. In your notebook, write a new sentence using each word."

Whiteboard/PowerPoint Version: Either give students a word list to choose from, or for lower level classes, several sentences with a word bank. Have the students write the complete sentences in their notebooks.

Proofreading/Editing

Skills: Writing

Time: 5-10 minutes

Level: High-Beginner to Advanced

Materials: Worksheet/white-board

To keep proper grammar usage fresh in your students' minds, they should practice frequently. This doesn't need to be a full grammar lesson; a quick warm-up activity can do the trick. You can give your students a variety of errors to correct: word choice, word order, punctuation, capitalization, etc. They should write the sentences or passage correctly.

Teaching Tips:

Begin by asking your student a few review questions about whatever rules he/she is practicing. ("When do you use capital letters?" or "What is a run-on sentence? How can you fix it?")

Procedure:

1. In advance, prepare a worksheet. You could even take a previous workbook activity and reproduce it.

2. The sentences or passage should practice previously studied points of grammar by having errors of that sort: word choice, word order, punctuation, capitalization, etc.

3. Have the students correct the errors.

Puzzles

Skills: Reading/Writing

Time: 10-30 minutes

Level: Beginner to Intermediate

Materials: A puzzle

Puzzles are an excellent way to review vocabulary and I find that most students enjoy doing them, particularly teenagers. They can also work very well for "quiet" classes that don't have a lot of outgoing students in them where it's hard to do some of the more active games like charades. It's really easy to make puzzles yourself using something like Discovery.com's Puzzlemaker (www.discoveryeducation.com/free-puzzlemaker) and it's actually the preferable option since you can include all the specific vocabulary that you'd like. I prefer to use the criss-cross option because it has the most educational benefit since it deals with meanings as well as vocabulary words.

Teaching Tips:

It's up to you whether or not to allow dictionaries or textbooks. In my experience, dictionaries don't really help that much while the course book where the words came from really does. You could also say that for the first five minutes, they must only use their brains, but they can use anything they want after that. If there is a particularly hard one that no student is able to get, I'll give the entire class a hint.

Procedure:

1. Go to Discovery.com and find the puzzlemaker.

2. Design your puzzle (criss-cross is best!), using words and definitions. Alternatively, you could give hints about the word related to the context you'd use it in instead of the actual definition. Here are two examples:

This animal has black and white stripes (skunk).

If a _____ sprays you, you'll smell really bad (skunk).

3. Have students complete the puzzle. I usually make it a bit competitive by putting them in pairs and awarding the first couple of teams a prize of some sort.

4. It's up to you whether or not to allow dictionaries or textbooks. In my experience, dictionaries don't really help that much while the course book where the words came from really does. You could also say that for the first five minutes, they must only use their brains,

but they can use anything they want after that. If there is a particularly hard one that no student is able to get, I'll give the entire class a hint.

Scaffolded Writing Prompts

Skill: Writing

Time: 10+ minutes

Level: Beginner to Intermediate

Materials: Scaffolded prompts

You may often be required to have students write beyond their actual level. The fastest way to get them from where they are to where you are required to take them is to provide scaffolded writing prompts. The level of scaffolding will depend on their level and the level of writing expected.

For your lowest-level students, this will look a lot like MadLibs. You will provide the bulk of the text, and they will make additions from choices you also provide. Toward the other end of the spectrum, you can provide example test essays with connectors and hedges removed, so they can practice using those correctly. For a greater challenge, you could provide the first sentence of each paragraph in an essay, and have the students complete the essay.

A basic high-beginner scaffolded writing activity I do is give students a journal prompt with a mind map which I have started for them. Depending on the prompt, I will create several lists on the mind map and fill in at least one example on each list. I may also include a list of useful words related to the topic. Students begin by filling in their mind map, then write their journal. This helps them think through what they want to say and helps them create a cohesive, understandable journal entry.

Procedure:

1. In advance, create a scaffolded writing prompt for your students. Depending on their level,

this may include useful vocabulary, a mind map or similar pre-writing task, and/or a partially written text.

2. Have students begin by filling in any pre-writing task, then complete the main writing activity.

Synonym/Antonym Brainstorm Race

Skill: Writing
Time: 5 minutes
Level: High-Beginner to Advanced
Materials: Large paper (one piece per group) or whiteboard and markers (at least one per group)

This is similar to the Review Race, but is used with new vocabulary, after introducing the terms and definitions. To play, divide students into groups of 4-5 and give each group at least one marker. If you are not using the whiteboard, also give each group one piece of A3 or butcher paper. Give students a time limit of 2-3 minutes to list all of the vocabulary words they can remember from the previous lesson. With higher-level classes, have students add a synonym, antonym, or brief definition. The group with the most correct words wins.

Procedure:

1. In advance, prepare markers and optionally, a piece of A3 or butcher paper for each group.
2. Divide students into groups of 4-5.
3. Have students work together to list all of the vocabulary and add at least one synonym and antonym of each word.
4. The group with the most correct words wins.

Vocabulary Square

Skill: Writing
Time: 20+ minutes

Level: High-Beginner to Advanced

Materials: Index cards (students should be told in advance to bring one card per vocabulary word); dictionary or textbook with glossary

This is a class activity to facilitate self-study as well as dictionary skills. Many students these days rely on their electronic dictionaries for translations and don't develop their English-English dictionary skills. They may also not realize the benefits of flashcards for vocabulary self-study. Regular repetition of exposure to new words is necessary to commit them to working memory.

It is an easy activity to set up. Have students divide their index into four corners:

1. Write the meaning in the students' own words.

2. Write at least one synonym and one antonym.

3. Write an example sentence.

4. Draw an image representing the term.

Remind students to review the flashcards at least once a day.

Teaching Tips:

You may want to complete a few examples together to remind students to restate the definitions rather than copying them. A PowerPoint of a completed index card will help students more easily understand the task. You could also draw an example on the whiteboard.

Procedure:

1. At least one class in advance, ask students to bring index cards. Alternatively, you can cut copy paper into 8 pieces, but it is not as durable.

2. Explain to students that flashcards are a great way to learn new vocabulary if they review the cards often.

3. Have students divide their index cards into four corners, and fill as follows:

1. Write the meaning in the students' own words.

2. Write at least one synonym and one antonym.

3. Write an example sentence.

4. Draw an image representing the term.

Word of the Day

Skills: Writing

Time: 5 minutes

Level: Beginner to Advanced

Materials: Whiteboard/PowerPoint

      I have frequently been required to either give my students a word, quote, or idiom of the day, outside of our usual text, but it's usually related to the text or a monthly theme. You can easily start a Word of the Day activity for your students, by giving them a single word each day from their text (but not a vocabulary word), current events or by having a theme for each month.

      Write the word on the whiteboard or PowerPoint along with the definition, part of speech, and several example sentences. Have students copy all of this in their notebooks in a section for their Words of the Day. You can use the word as an exit ticket, have a weekly quiz, or add one or two words to each regular vocabulary quiz.

Variation (more advanced): Idiom of the Day is where you give students an idiom with a definition and a picture (if possible). Have them make 1-3 sentences using it correctly.

Procedure:

1. In advance, prepare a collection of words from your students' textbook but not part of the vocabulary list.

2. Begin each day (or one day per week) with one new word. Introduce the word just as you would their regular vocabulary: present the word, the definition, part of speech and several example sentences.

3. Have students copy the sentences in the notebooks and add their own sentence.

4. Add all or some Words of the Day to your regular vocabulary quizzes.

Icebreaker/Warm-up

2 Truths and a Lie

Skills: Writing/Reading/Listening/Speaking

Time: 20-30 minutes

Level: Intermediate to Advanced

Materials: None

Play in groups of 4-6 in a bigger class, or everyone together in a small class. My general rule is that if you allow minimal or no follow-up questions, it takes around 3-4 minutes per student. However, if you allow 2-3 minutes of questions, it takes about 6-7 minutes per student. It's a good activity to use "always, usually, sometimes, never" or "can, can't" and "I've." Students write three sentences, one of which is false. They read their sentences and the other students guess the false one. Higher level classes can ask three questions, or question the person for a pre-determined amount of time (2-3 minutes) to determine the false one. A correct guess gets one point. Each student gets a turn to play.

Teaching Tips:

This is a useful activity for practicing the speaking sub-skills of initiating a conversation and responding to something in a questioning way. For example, students will have to say something like, "So you can make/play/do _____? I kind of don't believe you! Tell me _____" if you allow question time.

You can do this as a single activity in one class, or you can also do it over a series of days. For example, I taught at a winter camp where I had the same group of students for 10 days in a row. My class had 20 students, so as a warm-up for each day, 2 students had to go in the "hot-seat" (one at a time) and we got to ask the students questions about their 2 truths and 1 lie for three minutes. I appointed a "captain" to keep track of the points throughout the two weeks. The two winners got a $5 *Starbucks* gift certificate, which was a small way to add some *friendly* competition to the class.

You can also give points to the student in the hot-seat for anyone who doesn't figure out the correct answer. But, either do this or the other way I mentioned above. If you do both, it gets complicated and confusing very quickly!

Emphasize that students must pick things that are "big picture" ideas. The terrible examples I give are things like birthdays, hospital they were born in, name of sister, etc. There is simply no way to verify this information through asking any sort of interesting questions. Better categories are things like hobbies, travel, part-time jobs, skills and abilities. I have students write down their statements and try to catch any of the bad ones before the game starts.

Procedure:

1. Write three sentences on the board about yourself: two are true and one is not.

2. Explain to students that they are to do the same for themselves.

3. Do your demonstration with one group. Read your sentences and those students can ask three questions (or have two minutes, etc.) to ask questions.

4. Each student in the group must choose for themselves which sentence is false. Reveal the answer and whoever guessed correctly gets a point.

5. The students play the game in small groups, making sure that each person gets a chance to share their three statements. You can help move the activity along by acting as a time-keeper by giving each student's turn a specific time limit.

Alphabet Game

Skills: Writing

Time: 5 minutes

Level: High-Beginner to Intermediate

Materials: None

This is a simple way to introduce a topic. Some examples include jobs, cities, animals, etc. Have pairs of students write down A~Z on one piece of paper. Give them 2-4 minutes to think of one word/letter that fits that certain category. I make a rule that they can't use proper nouns. If you want to increase the difficulty or if you have a small class, you can make a rule that if two teams have the same word it doesn't count. This forces students to think more creatively.

Example: Topic = animals

A. Alligator

B. Bat

C. Cat

Etc.

Procedure:

1. In pairs, students write down the alphabet on a piece of paper.

2. Give students a topic and a certain amount of time.

3. Students think of one word per letter about the topic.

4. Check who has the most words at the end of the allotted time. Option for small classes: don't count repeated words so students have to think more creatively.

Boggle

Skills: Writing

Time: 10 minutes

Level: High-Beginner to Intermediate

Materials: "Boggle" grid on PowerPoint, whiteboard or paper

You've probably played the word game Boggle before. You shake up the letters and then you have a certain amount of time to make some words with connecting letters. You can play it with your students but you don't need the actual Boggle game. Simply make up a grid on the whiteboard, PowerPoint or on a piece of paper. I make a 6x6 grid and put some obvious words in like the names of colors or animals, or the vocabulary that we've recently been studying. Then, students divide into pairs and have to make as many words as possible that are 4+ letters. You can give a bonus for longer words if you like. At the end, students count up how many points they have. You can double-check for any errors and then award a small prize to the winning team.

Procedure:

1. Prepare a "Boggle" grid.

2. Students divide into pairs and try to make as many words as possible with 4+ letters. Students cannot use the same letter in a single square twice within a single word.

3. Students add up points. The teacher checks the answers of the top two or three teams.

o	r	p	t	s	a
e	a	i	e	t	f
b	k	n	e	r	i
a	d	r	g	o	r
c	o	t	l	s	e
k	f	h	m	a	n

Some possible words from this board:

green, pink, rake, back, fire, fires, fast, road, rose

My World

Skills: Writing/Reading/Speaking/Listening

Time: 10-15 minutes

Level: Beginner to Advanced

Materials: None

This is an excellent icebreaker activity that you can do on the first day of class to introduce yourself and then have the students get to know one or two of their classmates. You start by drawing a big circle on the whiteboard with the title, "My World." Inside the circle there are various words, pictures or numbers that have some meaning to you. For example, inside my circle there might be 1979, blue, 37, a picture of two cats, and a mountain. The students would then have to make some guesses about why these things are special to me. The correct answers are: my birth year, favorite color, number of countries I've been to, my pets, and hiking which is my favorite hobby.

Teaching Tips:

This is a good activity to practice some functional language dealing with correct or incorrect guesses. Teach your students how to say things like, "You're close," "Almost," "You got it," "That's right," "Really? No!"

Remember that the goal of our classes should be to make them more student-centered than teacher-centered, so try to minimize the amount of time that it takes for students to guess what's in your circle. Most of them are quite easy with only one or two more difficult ones. Then, if required, give your students some hints so they are able to get the harder ones. To increase student talking time, it's always better to have students playing this activity with each other instead of only with you.

For beginners, this activity might be a bit of challenge. You could write down these question forms to help them out:

Is this your _____ (hobby, birth year, age, favorite color)?

Do you have */a/an _____ (cat, three family members, etc.)?

Have you _____ (visited, gone to, tried, etc.)?

Procedure:

1. Draw a big circle on the board and write "My World" at the top. Put in some words, pictures

or numbers inside the circle that have some meaning to you.

2. Have students guess what each thing means. Give hints if necessary.

3. Students prepare their own "world."

4. Students can play with a partner or in small groups of 3-4.

Odd One Out

Skills: Reading/Speaking or writing

Time: 5 minutes

Level: Beginner to Intermediate

Materials: Groups of words

You can use Odd One Out to review vocabulary from the previous classes. Write up a few sets of vocabulary words on the whiteboard. I use four in one group, with one of them being the odd one out. For example: orange, cucumber, apple, banana. Cucumber is the odd one out because it's not a fruit.

Procedure:

1. Make 4-6 groups of four words, with one of them being unlike the others.

2. Put students in pairs and have them choose the odd word from each group and also write (or say) why they chose it. For example: Cucumber—not a fruit.

Review Race

Skill: Writing

Time: 5 minutes

Level: Beginner to Intermediate

Materials: Butcher or A3 paper (one piece per group) or whiteboard and markers (at least one per group)

Some students tend to look at each lesson as a discrete unit, forgetting that they are parts of a whole. This activity gets them using what they have learned. It's a great warm up activity. I've also used it before a test, both to boost their confidence and to give them one last bit of review time.

To play, divide students into groups of 4-5 and give each group at least one marker. If you are not using the whiteboard, also give each group one piece of A3 or butcher paper. Give students a time limit of 2-3 minutes to list all of the vocabulary words they can remember from the previous lesson. With higher-level classes, have students add a synonym, antonym, or brief definition. The group with the most correct words wins.

Procedure:

1. In advance, prepare markers, and optionally, a piece of A3 or butcher paper for each group.

2. Divide students into groups of 4-5.

3. Have students work together to list all of the vocabulary they can remember from the previous lesson within the time limit of 2-3 minutes.

4. For higher-level classes, have students add a synonym, antonym or brief definition of each word.

5. The group with the most correct words wins.

The "Expert" Conversation Activity

Skills: Speaking/Listening

Time Required: 20-30 minutes

Level: Intermediate to Advanced

Materials: None

Students write down five things that they're an expert in. Once they've written their lists, they circle the three that they think will be most interesting to other students in the class. Next, divide the students up into pairs and give them about 5-6 minutes to ask some questions to their partner about things they are experts in. Keep changing partners for as long as you want the activity to last, but more than 3-4 times gets kind of boring.

Teaching Tips:

This is a particularly useful activity for practicing many of the speaking sub-skills such as initiating a conversation, turn-taking, and appropriate length of responses. You can pre-teach some of these things before you begin the activity. For example, show your students how to initiate a conversation by saying something like, "I see you're interested in _____. What/where/why/when/who/how _____?"

Or you could teach your students about appropriate length of responses by doing one bad example and then one good example. Continue with the bad example by rambling on and on until the students are feeling a little bit uncomfortable and they'll see clearly what you mean.

If possible, try to get students to talk to someone that they don't know. This is particularly helpful for the students who don't know anybody else in the class, or don't have a friend. Having a five minute conversation with someone makes you feel like you actually know them and these students won't be so alone in future classes. I do this by asking students to choose partners whose names they don't know.

Procedure:

1. Talk about what "expert" means with your students. Tell them five things that you're an expert in.

2. Students make a list of 5 items.

3. Students choose the three things that they think will be most interesting to the others in the class. Tell students to do the same with their own lists.

4. Students find a partner and talk together for 5-6 minutes about the chosen topics. Starting the conversation, turn-taking and changing topics is up to them.

5. Students switch partners and continue.

Toilet Paper Icebreaker

Skills: Speaking/Listening

Time: 5-10 minutes

Level: Beginner to Advanced

Materials: Toilet paper

This is an icebreaker activity for the first day of class so that you can help the students get to know each other in a fun way. Bring in a roll of toilet paper, and depending on the size of your class, tell the students they can take a certain number of pieces (4-7 works well). You can also play this game with a bag of wrapped candies (wrapped for sanitary reasons) and as the student completes each speaking task, they can eat the candy. In fact, maybe all your classes would like this option better but it depends on your budget! Don't give them any other information.

Once everyone has their papers, explain that they have to tell the class one thing about themselves for each square of paper they have. For each sentence, they "throw-away" one square until they're done. If you have an extremely large class, you can put the students in groups of 5-6 for this activity instead of playing all together as you would for a smaller class.

Teaching Tips:

Students are always so curious about why they have a choice for how many they chose. Be mysterious and don't give away the secret until everyone has chosen.

Procedure:

1. Divide the students into groups of 5-6 (larger classes), or play together for a smaller class.

2. Students choose the number of pieces of toilet paper that they want depending on your minimum and maximum criteria.

3. Tell the students that for each square they took, they must say one interesting thing about themselves.

4. The first student says one thing about themselves and discards that square into the pile in the middle (or eats the candy!). The other students could make a response of some sort such

as "Me too," or "Really?", or "I can't believe it!" The second student says one thing and discards a square. Continue in a circle until all squares are used up.

5. An optional, but fun variation for higher level students is that they can have a chance to ask a follow-up question after each statement, but only one and the fastest person gets to do it. For each follow-up question, they can discard a square into the pile.

Words in Words

Skills: Writing

Time: 5-10 minutes

Level: Beginner to Intermediate

Materials: Worksheet/whiteboard or PowerPoint

You probably did this when you were in school. Give students a word and have them make as many words as possible using the letters in that word. For example: "vacation" = a, on, no, act, action, taco, ant, van. You can give a point for each word, so that the student with the most words wins, or give more points for longer words. When time is up (about five minutes), show students the possible answers.

Wordles.com has a tool that allows you to type in a word and get the possible words. For vacation, they listed 45 words, some of which I should have thought of myself and some of which are "Scrabble words." Since your students will not possibly know all of these words, it is up to you whether you show all the answers or an abridged list.

Procedure:

1. In advance, prepare a long word and write it on the whiteboard or a PowerPoint or give students individual worksheets.

2. Give students a time limit of about five minutes to make words from the letters in the word.

3. To make it a competition, when time is up, you can give students points for each word.

4. When the activity is finished, show students all of the possible words they could have made. You can get these from www.wordles.com.

Before You Go

If you found 101 ESL Activities: For Teenagers and Adults useful, please head on over to Amazon and leave a review. It will help other teachers like you find the book. Also be sure to check out our other books on Amazon at www.amazon.com/author/jackiebolen.

Printed in France by Amazon
Brétigny-sur-Orge, FR

13849999R00083